INVESTING
IN REAL ESTATE

INVESTING
IN REAL ESTATE

ANDREW JAMES McLEAN

WILEY

JOHN WILEY & SONS

New York · Chichester · Brisbane · Toronto · Singapore

Library of Congress Cataloging in Publication Date:

McLean, Andrew James.
   Investing in real estate / Andrew McLean.
     p.   cm.
   Bibliography: p.
   Includes index.
   1. Real estate investment—United States.   I. Title.
HD1382.5.M318   1988
332.63'24—dc 19

ISBN 0-471-60921-8 (cloth)
ISBN 0-471-60115-2 (pbk)

Printed in the United States of America

10 9 8 7 6

My thanks to Steve Trebbin and Vivian and Paul Schneider. A special thanks to Mike Hamilton whose idea gave this work inspiration.

PREFACE

Unlike other books on real estate, this text provides you with a broad, yet complete, topical guide to investing in real estate. It is concise, yet thorough, spanning a wide range of topics. I hope the reader will find it informative and interesting.

Everything from what to look for, how to buy it, what to do with it once you've got it, and how to sell it are included. Along the way you will be directed to specific techniques and methods, such as how to buy foreclosures and HUD property and the interesting, and best of all concepts, of lease option.

This text is unique because it features a simple and complete look at the latest changes in tax laws regarding real estate. It will teach you to be tax wise and dollar smart. That's right, the latest information on new tax rules and how they affect real estate are included. Dramatic changes in the Tax Reform Act of 1986 have severely altered the entire real estate industry, and you should be informed of what you can or cannot do according to the new law.

It also features how to successfully negotiate a good buy when renting or selling your property, with or without the services of an agent. Essentially, then, it is a do-it-yourself guide to everything you need to know about real estate. Step by step you will be informed of the right way to do things. Also provided are specific forms, such as leases, income and expense records, and a portfolio of other required forms to assist you along the path to profitable real estate investment.

This book is written in what I hope to be a clear and concise manner. It is intended as a guide for first-time home buyers and real estate professionals alike. Both will find it very useful and educational, while at the same time enlightening. I have flavored the text with a dash of my personal experience in real estate, which I trust will be beneficial.

The techniques I used may clarify what others tend to complicate. Through my own past achievements, as well as pitfalls, I endeavored to make this book the only one you will ever need regarding real estate investments.

Whether you are buying your first home or are in the process of exchanging numerous properties for a large multi-unit complex, this handbook was written especially for you.

Happy investing for both fun and profit,

A. J. McLean

AUTHOR'S NOTE

For clarity, I use masculine pronouns throughout the text. Sexism is neither intended nor implied. For simplicity, I use the term "mortgage" in this text, instead of continually describing both it and a trust deed. For all practical purposes, these instruments are similar, the only major difference being how they are enforced during foreclosure proceedings.

Furthermore, in the overall preparation of this book, I have endeavored to give good, sound advice at profitable strategy while investing in real estate. Although I have made every effort to provide completeness and accuracy to this work, the area of real estate is too rapidly changing, especially the tax laws, to guarantee such things. By no means am I rendering legal, accounting, or other professional service. Every transaction is different. Thus, no general book on such an expansive topic could address every situation. Therefore, you should consult a professional who is knowledgeable in local laws, accounting, and taxes before you act.

CONTENTS

1 INTRODUCTION: WHY REAL ESTATE INVESTMENT IS BEST FOR YOU

Why real estate as an investment? A question often asked but seldom fully explained or adequately answered. The answer is, in simple terms, that there is no better investment available, no other investment over which you can have such total control.

I believe the word "control" is very important here. I'm sure you're aware of the many investment scandals that have recently surfaced where a group of professional athletes were swindled out of millions of dollars by certain larcenous investment counselors. These innocent investors allowed their hard-earned funds to be invested through a third-party agent, thereby having no control whatsoever and putting total trust in someone else to invest their money. The results arose from the compound mistake of having given up control by placing trust in a third party and by this so-called investment adviser's probably investing the funds in the volatile securities market where, once again, the investor lost control of the outcome.

Let's face it, the stock market is probably the closest thing to shooting dice in a crap game, while the public at large usually craps out. Prices fluctuate daily while scandals of insider trading surface routinely. Sure, there are a select few shrewd investors who do very well in the stock market, but how does the public really fare when the closing bell finally rings?

On the other hand, real estate is available for the everyday working person to invest in, and to profit in without investment advisers. And, more than anything else, the real estate investor will have total control over his investments in historically stable markets.

But even real estate is cyclical. Its value will fluctuate with general economic conditions, however over the long term, virtually every well located property endures these up- and down swings and appreciates

1

in value. Inflation accounts for most of this increase in value, but another contributing factor is real estate's unique characteristic of increasing demand caused by new and increasing population and its limited supply (they just aren't making any more land).

You need real estate. You need protection from excessive income taxes and a shield from the eroding effects of inflation on your hard-earned income. You also need additional income and a sound method to develop financial security for you and your family. Real estate offers you all this, plus tax shelter capabilities that other common forms of investment do not. And, much more importantly, it offers you control over your own investment destiny. You will no longer need third-party advisers, whose judgment might be unsound, to make investments for you in volatile markets where you have no control.

Financially speaking, it's definitely a tough world out there, especially for someone with a growing family and who's working for someone else. You need an investment vehicle which will enable you to obtain a certain amount of financial security for those retirement years. As a famous saying goes, "A journey of a thousand miles must begin with a single step." Investing in your first home can be that first step, which can lead to other income-producing properties. And, eventually, through perseverance and experience, you can then consider becoming a full-time investor.

You actually don't need much to get started. Often, all that is required is a few thousand dollars. You don't need a college degree or a real estate license, you don't even need good credit or a high school diploma. What you do need is the motivation and the perseverance to apply what you're about to learn in this handbook to actual practice.

This is not a get-rich scheme where millions are made overnight. It's actually a slow methodical way of acquiring first one property, fixing it up, then renting or selling it in contemplation of acquiring additional properties. Some might call it a pyramid investment plan since you first acquire one property, increase its value, while at the same time sheltering existing income, thus allowing you more surplus income to invest in more properties. Then, you use income generated from the initial property to acquire additional investments.

HOW I GOT STARTED

During my senior year at Michigan State University, my dear grandmother passed away at the age of 72 and left me part of her modest estate. My share of the inheritance came to $11,000, to be exact. This amount of money may not seem like much to some of you, but to me it represented the opportunity of a lifetime, and I was extremely grateful. At that particular time in my life I was studying financial analysis, with the objective of becoming a stockbroker. But now, with this working capital available, I could begin speculating in the market with my own funds. And, if successful, I could continue to invest in the market and avoid the unsavory thought of working for someone else.

I began by plunging my entire inheritance, along with a margin account so I could purchase twice as much stock, into the stock market. (A margin account, in case you don't already know, is borrowing money from the broker to purchase more stock.) Well, investing on margin is just dandy when your stock is appreciating in value. However, if the negative aspects of investing occur, then your broker requires that you add more money to your margin account to make up for the deficit. If you don't have the money available to supplement your margin account, then your stock is sold (usually at a loss) to pay back the borrowed funds.

Needless to say, I got caught up in the frenzy of speculating just when the market and my stocks were going in the opposite direction of what I had predicted. The result of this fiasco was that in six months' time I had cut my inheritance in half. My hopes and dreams of becoming an independent stock investor were doomed. The experience was so exasperating that an alternative of becoming a stockbroker also seemed hopeless. (How could I possibly consider becoming a stockbroker, suggesting stocks for others to buy, when I was not even capable of making a profit for myself?) So I took what was left, approximately $5,500, and purchased a home in Lansing, Michigan.

Back in those days when I first started in real estate, I would buy old klunkers, fix them up and put renters in them, then later sell for a profit. This procedure of buy, fix-up, then sell seemed adequate at the time. However, over the years I learned a few tricks which helped to make this procedure more lucrative, less time consuming, and almost hassle-free.

The major disadvantage I found to this method of investment was the fact that after the fixer-upper was sold for a profit, I had to find another property to invest the proceeds in. (How to overcome this objectionable situation was solved later on when I moved to Las Vegas.)

It is a major disadvantage when you sell a profitable investment because, first of all, you have to take the time to locate, purchase, fix it up, then find a tenant for it. Then, when it's time to sell, a costly sales commission would usually be required to consummate the sale. All these procedures are very time consuming, especially when you're working full time at another profession.

After relocating to Las Vegas, I had purchased a small two-bedroom, one-bath home near downtown (in Biltmore). Once it was renovated and rented out, I noticed that over a two-year period the average stay of my tenants was six months, and I was getting tired of renting, then re-renting the same house over and over again. When it became vacant again in the Spring of 1983, I decided to advertise the property as a rental with an option to buy.

Immediately, the advertisement in the local paper received ten times the response the rent-only ad received. Within a week it was lease-optioned for $550 per month, and has been ever since. (While the property was rented only, it merely generated $410 per month in rent; $140 in additional income is only one of the advantages I discovered in lease-optioning this property.)

Under the lease-option method, I essentially developed an installment sale, which meant that I would receive income on this particular investment for the next 20 years. In addition, I wouldn't have to pay a sales commission to sell the property. I also discovered that option-to-buy occupants take much better care of property than do renting tenants. Furthermore, if I had sold the property outright, I would have had to have found another property to invest the proceeds in. Finally, this method offers tax advantages and several other benefits that will be discussed in more detail later in the text.

Today that house is worth twice what I paid for it. There are several reasons why this property turned out to be such a sound investment. First of all, it had a good location in a stable neighborhood near downtown Las Vegas. (Downtown casino employees could easily walk a few blocks to work.) Second, I had purchased it at a bargain price with a small down payment and had assumed the existing loan at an interest rate substantially below the prevailing market rate. Third, although it needed $1,200 in repair to get it in habitable condition, it was in sound condition, with many appealing features. And, last of all, it steadily increased in value over the years. The bottom line is that this property has given a great return on investment over the years and the tax shelter benefit was a giant bonus.

Let's look at an example of this investment in more detail to discover what I mean.

BILTMORE INVESTMENT EXAMPLE

Purchase price		$37,000
Cost to renovate		1,200
Down payment		4,500
Loans: First mortgage at 7%		15,500
Second at 10% interest only		17,000
Payments on first loan,		
including taxes and insurance	$150	
Payments on second loan	143	
Total payments	$293	

Property is lease-optioned at $550 per month, which yields a positive cash flow of $257 per month ($550 − 293 = 257) without considering $48 per month in equity build-up. Let's examine this example further on an annual basis.

Gross annual rental income	$550 × 12	$6,600
Less expenses		
Vacancy and credit loss (5%)	330	
Maintenance (5%)	330	
Loan payments ($293 − 48) =	245 × 12 = 2,940	
including taxes and insurance		
Total expenses	3,600	3,600
Net income before taxes		3,000

Now I can figure my return on investment. My gross income was $6,600 less total expenditures of $3,600, for a net profit, before taxes, of $3,000. Notice I said before taxes! Here is the golden bonus Uncle Sam allows to privileged real estate owners—*depreciation*. Depreciation is the legitimate tax shelter the government grants to income property owners.

By definition, depreciation is strictly a bookkeeping tax deduction allowance given to income property owners for wear and tear and obsolescence. It is not an out-of-pocket expense, such as taxes and insurance.

Now, in the preceding example, we have a net profit of $3,000 before taxes. I can now deduct a depreciation expense to offset this $3,000 net profit, and in most cases actually show a paper loss, for tax purposes, when actually we netted a $3,000 profit. Hence, the term "tax shelter" evolved, because the actual loss we realized for tax purposes can, in most cases, be applied against other forms of income.

In fact, what the actual tax law says is that you must depreciate a building for tax purposes, even though in reality the entire property is actually appreciating in value. The final result is that in most cases the value of the property is rising, while depreciable book value is dropping, and sheltering all the income realized from it. What more could you ask for?

Where can you find another investment that appreciates in value and gives you tax-free income at the same time? What's even greater is that the tax loss you realize can often offset other forms of income. It's surely the most lucrative tax incentive one could have.

THE PLAN IN A NUTSHELL

Fix-up properties offer the best opportunities, especially for the lay investor. A fix-up property, commonly referred to as a "fixer-upper," is a property in disrepair which can be purchased at a bargain price, renovated to create value through improvement, and then sold at a profit.

Essentially, you will be doing what millions of merchants and retailers have done for ages, that of purchasing a product wholesale, repackaging it, then earning a profit when it's sold at retail. This is of course an oversimplification, but it's true. In reality what you'll be doing is as follows: Make a good buy; fix it up, making the sales price, financing, and the entire property appealing; then sell it outright or on installment for a well-earned profit, realizing dividends for the next 20 years. These monthly dividends (plus additional tax savings you receive from owning income property) are reinvested into a second property as you continue to buy, fix up and sell; buy, fix up and sell, and so on.

You will be offered numerous money-making techniques in this investor's guide, and every one has proved successful, some more than others. The featured money-making technique will be lease option. This method has proved itself over the years to be the most profitable and hassle-free way for the novice investors to get the most for their money.

The contents of this book will help any investor, professional and/ or amateur. Complicated subjects are deciphered and converted into easy reading and instruction. All the concepts presented in this text have been tried and tested, and they work. What is required from you is to study the material then implement the concepts.

I recommend that if you're entirely new to real estate investment, glance through a few chapters and familiarize yourself with the terminology in the glossary first, then thoroughly read the entire book. If you properly implement the concepts presented and continue to persevere at real estate investment, within a reasonable amount of time you will have earned yourself the financial security associated with a rewarding portfolio of income-producing real estate.

2 FINANCING: THE KEY TO SUCCESSFUL INVESTING

In today's sophisticated real estate market there are a variety of methods to finance your real estate purchases. These include the ease, simplicity, and cost effectiveness of loan assumption as well as the very risky and unpredictable adjustable rate mortgages (ARMs). Also there are the popular government-sponsored programs of the VA and FHA, and, of course, the standard conventional loan. We will discuss the pros and cons of each method of financing to enable you to select the method best suited to your particular needs.

It is important that you grasp the fundamentals of real estate financing and its associated debt and not be apprehensive about incurring such debt on your real estate holdings. Large amounts of mortgage debt on real estate are essential to produce high yields and growth for the investor. As long as each property purchased generates more income than it costs to operate, all debt will be manageable.

Some real estate investors, especially those senior citizens with a conservative nature, think the best way to buy real estate is by using all cash without any financing whatsoever. This might have been the correct thinking during the 1920s and 1930s when the rate of inflation was negligible; but in today's highly inflationary economy, paying all cash for real estate is probably the most ill-advised choice an investor could make, since there are tremendous returns to be produced instead by leverage.

LEVERAGE

Leverage is the ability to use a small amount of cash to acquire a significant greater value in assets, such as real estate. Zero leverage would be a full-cash purchase, as opposed to a 10 percent down payment with 90 percent financing, which would be a purchase 90 percent leveraged. Due to the impact of inflation and appreciation on real estate values, getting as much leverage as you can when purchasing real estate offers you, the investor, a much greater yield on your invested dollars.

As a simple example of leverage, let's look at one particular real estate investment using 90 percent leverage with a 10 percent down payment, as opposed to purchasing the same property with zero leverage, or a full-cash purchase without financing. Suppose we purchase a property for $50,000 with a $5,000 down payment (10 percent), and a year later we realize an increase in value of 10 percent. Therefore, the property is now worth $55,000. Because we only put $5,000 down on the property and it appreciated $5,000, we realized a 100 percent return on investment. Now suppose we purchase the same property for $50,000 cash and similarly a year later the property appreciates to a value of $55,000. In this particular case our investment is $50,000, the appreciation factor is still $5,000, but the return is only a meager 10 percent on investment. When compared with the 100 percent return from the 10 percent down payment, it is easy to see the value of leverage. (About the only time a 100 percent cash-purchase price would be advantageous is when a property could be purchased substantially below market value. Then the buyer could refinance his cash purchase in order to recoup the majority of his cash investment.)

In order to succeed and profit at real estate investing one must view the financing of real estate as a joint venture with lenders. However, as the investor you don't have to share with the lender the profits realized; you are only required to pay lenders the interest on their money. In other words, the debt you incur on a particular property is not really a debt you will pay back with your own hard-earned money, but actually a debt that will generate income and appreciation and which you will pay back with a tenant's money after renting the property out and earning yourself a subsequent profit.

Keep in mind that even giant corporations, such as General Motors, which have an abundance of surplus cash, will always finance their real estate purchases so as to improve their return on investment through leverage.

FINANCIAL TERMINOLOGY

Before we get into the types and methods of financing real estate, you should familiarize yourself with the more common financial instruments and terms used in the industry today.

Mortgages and Deeds of Trusts

Mortgages and Deeds of Trusts are financial instruments that create liens against real property. These instruments state that, should the borrower default on the loan (fail to make payments when due), the lender has the legal right to sell the property in order to satisfy the loan obligation in a foreclosure sale.

There are two parties involved in a mortgage: the *Mortgagor*, or the borrower and property owner, and the *Mortgagee*, or the lender. There are also two parts to a mortgage: the *Mortgage Note*, which is evidence of the debt, and the *Mortgage Contract*, which is the security for the debt. The note promises to repay the loan, while the contract promises to convey title of the property to the mortgagee in case of default.

Trust Deeds are similar to mortgages except that an additional third party is involved and the foreclosure procedures are more simplified. Under a trust deed the borrower, or the owner, is called the *Trustor*.

The lender is called the *Beneficiary*. The intermediate third party, whose responsibility is to hold title to the property for the security of the lender, is referred to as the *Trustee*.

Under a trust deed, if the trustor defaults on the loan obligation, the subject property will be sold at public auction by the trustee through provisions in the "power of sale" clause contained in the trust deed, without court procedure.

Foreclosure is initiated by a notice of default, which is recorded by the trustee with a copy sent to the trustor. If after three months the trustor does nothing to remedy the situation, a notice of sale is posted on the property, and advertisements of the sale are carried in local newspapers once a week for three weeks. If during this period the trustor fails to pay the beneficiary sufficient funds to halt the foreclosure, the sale will be conducted by the trustee. Proceeds from the foreclosure sale are first disbursed to the beneficiary, then to any other lien holders according to their priority.

Foreclosure under a mortgage instrument, as opposed to a trust deed, is notably longer (periods in excess of a year are common). It is for this reason that more than half the states in the United States prefer the trust deed over a mortgage instrument.

Second trust deeds and mortgages are similar to firsts, except that they are second in priority to a first loan with respect to security and their ability to claim any proceeds through foreclosure.

Differences between Assumed, Subject-to, and Transferred Mortgages

There are important differences in the meaning of these terms. An *Assumed Mortgage* occurs when the borrower assumes the legal loan obligation to make the loan payments, while the lender releases the previous borrower from the liability. Assumption then, technically speaking, can only legally take place in the absence of a due-on-sale clause.

Buying the property *Subject-To* the existing mortgage occurs when the buyer takes over the loan obligation without the existing borrower's being released from the liability, and without formal arrangement with the lender. Caution should be taken when buying property subject-to the existing mortgage—especially when a due-on-sale clause is involved—because the legality of enforcement of the due-on-sale clause differs in each state.

An *Assigned Mortgage* is one that you already own. It is an asset, or a note, that someone is paying you principal and interest on, and your security is the mortgage against certain property. As your down payment, you could assign this mortgage to the seller of the property you wish to acquire.

Finally, be aware of *Due-on-Sale* and *Alienation* clauses written into loan documents. Without going into great detail, they both essentially mean the same thing, that is, that if the title transfers to another party, the lender can call the total amount owed due and payable within 30 days. Or the lender has the right to ask for assumption fees and an increased rate of interest. FHA and VA loans do not have these clauses, which makes them very attractive, especially if the interest rate is below the market interest rate, and the fact that they are fully assumable in most cases, without any credit qualification whatsoever.

TYPES OF REAL ESTATE LOANS

Real estate loans can be classified in several different ways. One means of classification is according to the plan of repayment of the loan which the borrower and lender agree upon. The basic repayment plans available are:

- *Interest-only (Straight-term) loans*
- *Amortized loans*
- *Partially amortized loans*
- *Adjustable rate loans*
- *Graduated loans*

Interest-only Loans
Also referred to as the straight-term loan, this particular loan requires the payment of interest only during the term of the loan. At the end of

the term, the entire sum of principal is due and payable in one final balloon payment. For example, the annual payment schedule for an interest-only loan for $40,000 at 10 percent interest for a term of five years is as follows:

1st year $40,000 × .10 = $ 4,000 interest
2nd year $40,000 × .10 = $ 4,000 interest
3rd year $40,000 × .10 = $ 4,000 interest
4th year $40,000 × .10 = $ 4,000 interest
5th year $40,000 × .10 = $ 4,000 interest

$20,000 total interest paid
$40,000 balloon payment

$60,000 total principal and
        interest for 5 years

Prior to the Great Depression of 1929, the interest-only loan was the most common payment method for real estate financing. Many borrowers took out these loans for short terms expecting to renew them term after term, thus deferring payment of the principal almost indefinitely.

But the entire world economy failed during the Depression, and most lenders were unable to "roll over" or perpetuate these interest-only loans. The results were devastating. Lenders began calling loans, requiring the borrowers to pay the entire principal amount owing, which they did not have. Thus, lenders began foreclosing on these loans throughout the country.

The Great Depression made almost everyone, especially the financial industry, aware of the inherent dangers in this type of financing. A more practical form of loan soon materialized in the *Amortized Loan.*

Fully Amortized Loans

An alternative to the interest-only loan was the fully amortized loan, featuring equal payments over its term, which would consist of both principal and interest. In contrast to the interest-only loan, the fully amortized loan commonly has a longer term of 30 years or more and is completely paid off at the end of its term.

Initial payments on the amortized loan consist mostly of interest, but as the loan matures more of each payment is applied toward principal, since interest on an amortized loan is calculated on the loan's outstanding principal balance. Therefore, after each payment is made, the principal balance owing is reduced, resulting in a smaller interest portion and a larger principal portion of the overall payment.

Partially Amortized Loans
The partially amortized loan is similar to the fully amortized loan, except that a balloon will be left coming due at the end of the term. The purpose of this type of loan is to allow the borrower a smaller payment on the loan and to partially pay off the principal owing, thus reducing his regular monthly payment. This type of loan is popular when the seller finances his equity in the property under a purchase money second mortgage.

Adjustable Rate Loans
Adjustable rate mortgages (ARMs) originated a few years ago for the purpose of protecting long-term lenders from radical changes in market interest rates. Traditionally, conventional lenders were lending out their funds at reasonable interest rates, and rightly so as their cost of acquiring that money seldom fluctuated up or down. But along came the hyper-inflationary times of the mid-1970s and the 1980s, and the cost of money to lend out went up dramatically. At the same time these lenders had billions of dollars loaned out at interest rates substantially below what it cost them to acquire these funds. Thus, the arrival of the adjustable rate mortgage.

ARMs vary somewhat, but basically they are very similar in function. The initial rate of interest that the loan originated at is allowed to fluctuate over the entire term of the loan. Usually, if the interest rate originates at 9 percent, it is allowed to increase up to 6 points to a limit of 15 percent, with a maximum increase of 2 percent during any 12-month period. Typically, the amount of interest rate charged is tied to some government index, such as the prime rate. In other words, if the prime rate goes up, your ARM interest rate goes up, but not to exceed 2 points in one year, and not to exceed 6 points over the term of the loan.

Usually a borrower can originate an ARM at a lower interest rate than that of a conventional loan, mainly due to a lesser amount of risk realized by the lender. However, the borrower must realize that the interest rate of the ARM has the potential to increase 6 points over the term of the loan. For instance, on a loan of $80,000 at 8 percent for 30 years the principal and interest payment would be $587.02. For the same loan and term at 14 percent (the 6 percent maximum increase allowed), the principal and interest payment would be $947.90, or a monthly difference of $360.88. Over the entire term of 30 years, that's the difference of over $129,000. As you can see, ARMs represent a substantial and significant risk to the borrower, and it would be wise to avoid them at all costs.

A convertible ARM is the latest innovation in real estate financing. This is an ARM that can be changed quickly into a fixed-rate loan, with the lender setting certain limits at which the conversion can be made. At the time of this writing, initial offerings of the convertible ARM consisted of convertibility at a cost of $750 to a fixed rate during the first five years of the term of the loan. The initial rate of interest is 8.75 percent plus 2 points, compared with 10.5 percent plus 2 points on a 30-year fixed-rate loan.

Graduated Loans
Also known as the Graduated Payment Mortgage (GPM), this plan offers smaller initial loan payments which become larger as the term goes on. This type of loan anticipates the borrower's future ability to repay the loan in expectation of later income growth to meet the GPMs schedule of increasing payments.

LOAN UNDERWRITING

The process of risk evaluation is termed underwriting. Lending on real estate involves considerable amounts of money, and frequently the money a lender loans is not his own but rather borrowed money— money that is likely to be in a savings account entrusted to the lender's safekeeping. Therefore, it is very important that the lender carefully evaluate the risk before lending a considerable amount of money to just "anybody" to finance a specific property.

A loan underwriter must evaluate three basic items: the borrower, the property, and the location.

The borrower is required to fill out a standard loan application, which will include information about income and financial condition. From the loan application, the lender will evaluate the borrower's ability to repay the loan. In addition, the lender will order a credit report and an appraisal of the subject property.

Not only must the borrower demonstrate the ability to repay, he must show a desire to repay. From the credit report the borrower's credit history is brought to the attention of the lender. Past due bills, judgments, collection agency notices, foreclosure, and bankruptcy are all evidence of a borrower's poor credit.

Next the lender evaluates the security (collateral) for the loan, the property itself. The written appraisal is examined to determine the property's market value while a title report is ordered to uncover liens or other information against it.

Finally, the property's location is evaluated. The lender considers the presence of adequate utilities, street paving, and distance from shopping and recreational facilities. Proximity to schools and public transportation are also considered. Outside forces (economic obsolescence) that can cause a decline in the subject property's value are also evaluated. These can be anticipated negative changes, such as the intrusion of industrial developments into the area, declining values in the surrounding neighborhoods, or changes in zoning.

All these items have a bearing on the lender's final decision to approve or disapprove a loan, yet the amount of down payment invested by the borrower has to be finally considered. The smaller the down payment, the more money the lender has to lend, which means more risk for the lender and less risk for the borrower. Then, if the borrower defaults and the lender is forced to foreclose, there is a greater risk that the lender cannot recover the full interest in the property because of this smaller down payment.

Loan-to-Value Ratio

The customary term to describe a ratio or relationship between the amount of down payment and the value of the property is the loan-to-value ratio (LTVR). To calculate the LTVR, divide the loan amount by the property's appraised value or selling price, whichever is less. The resulting LTVR is expressed as a percentage, as follows:

Example of LTVR

In this example the loan amount is $60,000 and the appraised value is $75,000, however the property sold for $77,000. Therefore, to determine LTVR the loan amount is divided by appraised value, not the selling price which is more than the appraised value.

$$\frac{\$60,000}{\$75,000} = .80 = 80\% \text{ LTVR}$$

Discount Points

Both the Veterans' Administration (VA) and the Federal Housing Administration (FHA) set the maximum permissible interest rate that can be charged the buyer on their particular loans. Frequently this maximum rate is pegged below those interest rates charged by lenders in the open market. Therefore, in order to provide an incentive to originate VA and FHA loans, lenders are permitted to equalize the difference between this pegged rate and open market rates by charging discount points.

To calculate discount points, first deduct the VA or FHA rate from the open market interest rate. As an example, assume the following interest rates are in effect:

Open market interest rate	11.0%
FHA fixed interest rate	10.5%
Difference in rates	.5%

Based on past studies on the average life of a mortgage, it has been established that each 1 percent difference in interest rates equals 8 discount points. (A 1% difference equals 8/8 discount points). Thus, a .5 percent difference in interest rates equals 4/8. Therefore, each eighth represents 1 discount point. Then, to originate the loan from the above example, the lender would charge 4 points, or 4 percent of the loan amount.

Buyers under VA and FHA loan programs are not permitted to pay these discount points, and they are therefore paid by the seller. However, the lender is not prohibited from charging another form of points, termed service points, on all types of loans.

Similar to a discount point, a service point represents 1 percent of the loan amount. These service points, often referred to as loan origination fees, are incorporated into the loan with the purpose of increasing the lender's yield without raising the interest rate. Like interest rates, what lenders charge in service points tends to fluctuate according to supply and demand of money available to lend.

LOAN ASSUMPTION

Before we get into descriptions of the primary methods of creating new financing, the advantage of assuming low-interest rate existing loans has to be elaborated on. Existing VA and FHA loans (originated by previous owners), and in some cases existing conventional loans, are fully assumable without credit qualification. (Note: FHA loans funded after January 1, 1987, are assumable but require qualification by the new buyer. After two years have elapsed from loan origination date, they are fully assumable without credit qualification).

Furthermore, assumption is far less expensive and cumbersome than creating new financing under the other customary methods. Assumption of existing loans requires only a small assumption fee of $50, as opposed to excessive loan origination fees charged by conventional lenders. (Loan origination fees usually are 2 percent of the loan amount, thus a fee on a $100,000 loan would be a charge of $2,000.) Loan assumption also does not require the costs and related hassles of appraisals and credit reports (which can cost $150 and $50 respectively), and paid for by the borrower. That's right—no credit report, no excessive loan fees, no questions, and only a small assumption fee is charged to the borrower.

Not only is loan assumption attractive from a buyer's point of view, but as a seller you have a built-in advantage because the loan you assumed as the buyer is now fully assumable when you sell. Another advantage is that you can later "wrap" this existing loan when you sell at a much higher interest rate and make a profit on the spread in interest rates. (This concept of wrapping existing loans will be discussed further later in this chapter.)

Another advantage loan assumption has over other methods of financing is the fact that an assumption merely takes a few days to close, as opposed to from 60 to 90 days to conclude a transaction using other methods of financing. Although the VA, FHA, and conventional lenders definitely have their place in the real estate industry and are more often than not appreciated, it is their efficiency I question and criticize. When I say 60 to 90 days to close a real estate deal, I'm being conservative. I have had FHA deals take up to six months to close by the time all the bureaucrats quit fooling around with all their government red tape. These delays are very frustrating to investors and can easily be overcome by the smart investor who uses the ease, the simplicity, and the more profitable method of loan assumption.

PROGRAMS TO INSURE OR GUARANTEE LOANS

Real estate loans are divided into two categories: loans insured or guaranteed by the federal government (in some cases state government) and loans which are not. These loans without government support are termed conventional loans.

While programs under the Veterans' Administration were created to assist veteran home buyers, the Federal Housing Administration was created to assist both homeowners and lenders. During the troubled economic times of the 1930s, conventional lenders were made aware that an alternative to conventional lending practices was needed. Hence, the origin of the FHA.

The FHA not only pioneered loan insurance but also was instrumental in establishing uniform loan qualification standards for prospective borrowers.

The following material describes the available programs, beginning with the VA loan.

VA FINANCING

This program under the direction of the Veterans' Administration guarantees loans made by private lenders to eligible veterans. If no private financing is available, the VA will make direct loans to veterans.

The VA will guarantee loans on the following types of property: one- to four-family dwellings (fourplex), single-family dwellings (including condominiums), mobile homes, and mobile home lots.

Eligibility

Eligible veterans are those with a minimum of 90 days active duty in the armed forces during World War II (September 16, 1940, to July 25, 1947) or during the Korean War (June 27, 1950, to January 31, 1955). Veterans whose active duty transpired between July 25, 1947, and June 27, 1950, or any time after January 31, 1955, are required to have had a minimum of 180 days active duty. Unmarried spouses of veterans who served during the above periods and have service-related deaths are also eligible.

Among discharged veterans only those who were discharged under other than dishonorable conditions or because of service-connected disability are eligible.

In addition, certain citizens of the United States who served in the armed forces of an allied foreign government during World War II are eligible.

How to Apply

A veteran may apply for a Certificate of Eligibility at any regional VA office. This request should be accompanied by discharge papers (Form DD-214) or evidence of current active duty status.

Appraised Value

Once the eligible veteran locates the property that will accommodate VA financing, the VA will appraise the property and issue a Certificate of Reasonable Value (CRV). The amount of the loan guaranteed cannot exceed the CRV, including construction, alteration, or repairs.

Loan Guaranty

Currently there is no limitation on the amount of a loan eligible for a VA loan guaranty. However, there is a restriction on the amount of guaranty that can be issued.

The maximum guaranty for a loan to finance the purchase of a dwelling is 60 percent of the loan amount or $27,500, whichever is less, including construction or alteration costs of the dwelling. Generally, most lenders who fund VA loans will lend, with no down payment required, up to four times the amount of the guaranty. Therefore, $110,000 ($27,500 × 4) is the current maximum loan amount available with no down payment. Up to $135,000 can be borrowed in some cases, but a 25 percent down payment is required for any amount in excess of $110,000.

Also the same guaranty is authorized to refinance existing liens of record in owner-occupied homes by eligible veterans.

Buyer Qualification

VA guidelines recommend a limit of 41 percent of the gross monthly income to be paid toward total debt payments. Total debt payments include: mortgage payment (principal, interest, taxes, and insurance), consumer credit card payments, car payments, and assessments. The following guideline for buyer qualification is generally used by those lenders who fund VA loans: The monthly income of both husband and wife less their monthly debt payments should equal four times the total monthly payment of the purchased home. The veteran's job stability and credit-worthiness are considered along with present and anticipated income. Overtime pay is not taken into account for long-term projections to meet loan payments but is considered against short-term obligations. Furthermore, the VA does not accept co-signers and co-mortgagors.

Down Payment

The VA does not require a down payment by the veteran up to the maximum loan amount of $110,000. However, should the veteran agree to purchase a home in excess of this limit, a 25 percent down payment is required for any amount over $110,000.

Existing Loans

When a veteran is still liable for his previous VA loan (where he may still own his own home or has allowed a new buyer to assume the existing mortgage), the following is the method for computing the maximum VA loan the lender will make on a new home, based on the veteran's remaining entitlement.

The maximum loan is the equivalent entitlement plus 75 percent of the CRV or the purchase price, whichever is less. For example, assume a veteran bought a home in 1968 using the VA entitlement. (The maximum VA loan guaranty in 1968 was $12,500.) Then in 1979, that same veteran decided to rent his home and purchase a new home for $80,000 with a CRV equal to the purchase price. What is the maximum VA loan obtainable and how much of a down payment does he need to finance his new home?

Answer:	
Maximum loan guaranty in 1979	$25,000
Less maximum loan guaranty in 1968	12,500
Remaining veteran entitlement	12,500
Plus 75% of the $80,000 CRV	60,000
Equals maximum loan attainable	$72,500

Therefore, at a purchase price of $80,000 the veteran would need a cash down payment of $7,500.

Entitlement

The VA permits entire restoration of a veteran's full entitlement of the current maximum guarantee of $27,500, if the property has been sold and the previous loan has been paid in full. The veteran will also receive full entitlement should the property be sold to another veteran who assumes the existing VA loan with release of liability and agrees to use his own entitlement.

Even though a veteran may already have an existing VA loan, he can still purchase a new home without selling the old home as long as his entitlement varies substantially from his original entitlement. For example, if he bought the original home with a maximum loan guarantee of $7,500, the remaining entitlement would be $20,000, which is the difference between the current guaranty of $27,500 and the maximum of $7,500 at the time his original home was financed.

Occupancy Requirement

The veteran must sign a Certification of Intention to occupy the home he is about to purchase, which is required by the VA before the loan will be made. However, should the veteran later move to another home, he may rent his old home financed by the VA loan.

Closing Costs

Closing costs must be paid in cash at the close of escrow and cannot be included in the loan. VA Regulation 36:4312 prohibits excessive closing costs from being charged to the veteran buyer for the purchase, construction, repair, alteration, or improvement of residential property. This regulation prepares a schedule for allowable closing costs.

Points

When the market rate for interest is higher than the VA interest rate, the lender will not make the loan unless he is paid the difference in the form of a loan fee, referred to as points. Since the veteran buyer is only allowed to pay a maximum loan origination fee of 1 percent, the seller has to be charged points to consummate the transaction.

Impounds

VA requirements make it necessary for lenders to collect from the borrower funds to cover real estate taxes and hazard insurance premiums which is set aside in a reserve account referred to as "impounds." This amount will be prorated monthly and paid as part of the monthly mortgage payment.

Mobile Home Financing

The VA is authorized to guarantee loans made by private lenders to eligible veterans for the purchase of new or used mobile homes with or without a lot. The guaranty on a mobile home loan will be an amount equal to the veteran's available entitlement, not to exceed the maximum of $20,000 or 50 percent, whichever is less. A veteran who already owns a mobile home may obtain a VA-guaranteed loan to purchase a lot on which to place the mobile home.

Veterans who receive a guaranteed mobile home loan can use their full entitlement to buy a standard home if their mobile home loan is paid off in full.

VA interest rates for mobile home loans vary (they're usually higher) from those established for standard home loans.

Loan terms for the purchase of a new, single-wide mobile home, with or without a lot, or a loan to purchase a lot only, is limited to a maximum of 15 years and 32 days. A loan for a double-wide, new mobile home, with or without a lot, has a maximum term of 20 years and 32 days. The maximum term for used units may not exceed the preceding units or the remaining physical life of the unit as determined by the VA, whichever is less.

It is likely that the VA will establish maximum loans above these limits and to require the veteran to place a 10 percent down payment when purchasing a mobile home.

An approved mobile home must be: a minimum size of 40' × 10'; constructed for towing; equipped for year-round living; and conform to the specifications of the American National Standard Institute (ANSIO standard #A-119.1).

FHA FINANCING

The Federal Housing Administration, is a division of the U.S. Department of Housing and Urban Development. Loans made by the FHA insure full payment of the mortgage loan to the lender. The mortgage-insurance premium totaling 3.8 percent of the loan amount, is paid by the borrower in one of two ways: either the sum can be paid in full at closing, or it can be financed into the loan amount.

FHA guidelines require a limit of about 38 percent of the borrower's net monthly income for mortgage payments, which include principal and interest, real estate taxes, hazard insurance, and utility bills. A total of 53 percent of the net monthly income is allowed for total debts.

Currently the FHA's mortgage insurance limit is $67,500. Limits of up to $90,000 are generally made for areas designated by the FHA as "high-cost" areas. (At the time of this writing Congress was considering a bill with provisions raising the maximum limit to $101,250.)

Down-payment stipulations require the FHA buyer to place 3 percent down on the first $25,000 of the loan and 5 percent on the remaining amount borrowed.

FHA loans can be prepaid without penalty; however homeowners may be liable for one month's interest if a 30-day notice of intent to prepay is not submitted to the lender servicing the mortgage.

FHA loans are fully assumable, with one exception. FHA loans made after January 1, 1987, require that the assumptor's credit be reviewed if the loan being assumed is less than two years old and originated after January 1, 1987.

Other FHA Programs Available

Title II—Sec. 203(b). Finance the acquisition of one- to four-family dwellings, either proposed, under construction, or existing.

Title II—Sec. 203(b). Veterans. This program assists veterans in financing a single-family home, either existing, proposed, or under construction.

Title II—Sec. 207. Finance the acquisition of mobile home parks and rental housing.

Title II—Sec. 221(d)(2). Finance the acquisition of existing or proposed housing; or rehabilitate low cost, one- to four-family dwellings for displaced families; or finance one-family homes for low- or moderate-income families.

Title II—Sec. 221(d)(4). Finance the rehabilitation or construction of five or more dwelling units.

Title II—Sec. 222. Finance the acquisition of owner-occupied homes for service personnel.

Title II—Sec. 223(f). Finance the acquisition or the refinancing of existing multifamily dwellings.

Title II—Sec. 234(c). Finance the acquisition of individually owned condominium units.

Title II—Sec. 234(d). Finance the acquisition of condominiums and projects that will be converted to condos upon completion.

Title II—Sec. 235. To aid lower-income families by paying part of the family's mortgage-interest payment on low-cost homes, duplexes, or condos.

Title I— To finance the acquisition of mobile homes that must be used by the owner as principal residence.

CONVENTIONAL FINANCING

Beyond FHA and VA loan programs for originating new financing, there is the conventional loan. This is the primary method ᶜ non-veterans and those who wish to borrow more than the FHA limit. Conventional loans have stricter qualification requirements that vary with the amount of down payment. The lower the down payment, the tougher the restrictions.

Conventional loans usually require a 20 percent down payment. Anything less than 20 percent would require private mortgage insurance (PMI) to protect the lender from default. Even with PMI, the majority of conventional lenders would require a minimum of 10 percent down.

Qualifications for conventional loans vary, but most lenders have guidelines that no more than 25 percent of the borrower's gross monthly income can go toward the mortgage payment, and no more than 33 percent of their gross monthly income toward total debts.

Most conventional loans have prepayment penalties and are usually not assumable. In certain cases, some conventional loans are in fact assumable; however they usually require credit qualification by the assumptor.

How Much House Can You Afford?

How much house you can afford depends on the type of financing you choose. Originating new financing under FHA, VA, Conventional, or Adjustable Rate Mortgage all have different income and down-payment requirements. Originating new financing requires much more than good credit. Qualifying for a new loan also means you must meet certain income requirements to show the ability to pay back the loan. Essentially all these methods of financing require a range of from 25 to 41 percent of gross monthly income to be allocated for monthly mortgage payments. The higher percentage range allows for the payment of other debt obligations, including the mortgage payment.

Overall, the VA loan is the most liberal for the home buyer, as it offers the ability to purchase a home with no money down and at interest rates usually below the prevailing market interest rate. The FHA loan is the second most liberal, because it requires a small down payment—3 percent on the first $25,000 borrowed, and 5 percent on the remainder. The FHA loan interest rate is also favorable to conventional loan rates. Third in attractiveness would be the conventional loan, which in most cases requires a 20 percent down payment at an interest rate higher than that of the VA and FHA loans. A lesser down payment can be made under conventional terms; however private mortgage insurance is then required at a cost of one-quarter to one-half percent more in interest charges.

Last in priority of types of financing would be the Adjustable Rate Mortgage (ARM). These types of loans start the borrower off in the early years at a rate of interest usually significantly below that of the conventional rate, but gradually increase or decrease over the term of the loan.

The less stringent qualifications of loans backed by the federal government housing programs make them the most affordable, primarily because of lower down payment and income requirements.

ALTERNATIVE METHODS OF FINANCING

Besides the VA and FHA or conventional financing, the potential home buyer has several other methods available to finance a purchase. Under certain circumstances, the seller of the property can also be the lender, as when the property is sold under a wrap-around mortgage or land contract. The following material covers these unique methods of financing in addition to other secondary methods.

Wrap-around Mortgage

The wrap-around mortgage (Also referred to as an All-Inclusive Trust Deed, or AITD) is probably the most lucrative method of financing real estate available today. The wrap-around loan is used when the seller of real property wants to maintain the existing low-interest financing, so he "wraps" the existing loans with a new wrap-around loan at a higher interest rate. The seller continues making payments on the existing low-interest loans while the buyer makes payments to the seller on the new wrap-around loan. The seller would then earn a profit on the spread in interest rates. Here's how it works:

WRAP-AROUND LOAN EXAMPLE

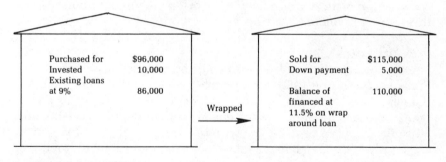

Purchased for	$96,000	
Invested	10,000	
Existing loans at 9%	86,000	

Wrapped →

Sold for	$115,000
Down payment	5,000
Balance of financed at 11.5% on wrap around loan	110,000

Seller pays out $850/mo.   Buyer pays out $1,050

In the preceding example, the seller creates and carries a new loan of $110,000 at 11.5 percent. Payments on the existing first and second loans are a total of $850 per month. Payments on the new wrap-around loan are $1,050 per month, therefore the seller earns a $200 per month profit.

As you can readily see, there are tremendous advantages to assuming existing low interest rate loans. Besides the cash savings in acquiring these loans, their flexibility allows you to wrap them and earn a handsome profit. Just the fact that you have all this built-in financing on the property is reason enough to avoid creating the other, more cumbersome forms of new financing.

Land Contract (Contract of Sale)

A land contract, sometimes referred to as a contract of sale or agreement of sale, is strictly a contract between buyer and seller without the involvement of a financial intermediary. Under a land contract a buyer would agree to purchase a property and pay principal and interest to the seller along with an optional down payment. Title to the property remains with the seller until conditions of the contract are fulfilled. The buyer retains possession of the property, however, so if the buyer should default on the agreement (not pay as agreed), the property would revert to the seller.

Similar to a wrap-around mortgage, land contracts are useful in "wrapping" existing low interest rate financing. The contract should stipulate that the buyer pays a certain fixed rate of interest, which is in fact higher than the combined rates on the existing loans.

Caution must be taken when structuring buyer and seller conditions in a land contract because the law covering this topic is vague, and the status of land contract sales vary from state to state. Therefore, consultation with a trusted attorney before involving yourself with this form of financing is advisable.

Equity Loans

Equity loans are essentially a loan made by a lender against the equity of his home. During 1987 they became the hottest financial product of the year, and with good reason. Because of the then-latest tax reform which will eventually exclude consumer interest as a tax deduction, an equity loan can provide you with sources of credit for which interest is fully tax deductible on your income tax return. In addition they usually offer interest rates that are more attractive than borrowing with credit cards.

The most common reference point for determining equity loan rates is about 3–4 points above the prevailing prime interest rate, which is set by the nation's largest banks. Currently the prime interest rate is 8.25 and has been below 10 for the past two years. However, the prime lending rate has been as high as 21.5 late in 1980. It is very unlikely we will see those days of a prime lending rate over 20, at least in the near future. But if you are interested in taking out an equity loan, be prepared for the worst. Three years down the road the prime rate could be 12 or 14. It would be wise to calculate what your payments would be under such circumstances. Before you borrow, be sure you know how much a variable rate can increase—and how often.

Tax Loophole for Equity Loans.   The Tax Reform Act of 1986 has created a loophole that is associated with equity loans. According to the new tax law, the consumer-interest deduction is being phased out over the next two years, yet certain equity loans are tax deductible. In other words, because of the new tax law, it would be reason enough just to take out an equity loan to pay off all existing consumer debt. This way you would pay off consumer debt, which is not tax deductible, with new equity debt, which is tax deductible.

Keep in mind that it would be unwise to consider a tax break alone as reason enough to borrow. Also keep in mind that new tax laws save no more than 15 cents on the dollar for some people, and a maximum of 28 cents on the dollar for others.

Purchase-Money Seconds

This is a method of financing in which the seller of the property takes back a loan for the equity in the property, instead of taking cash. For example, you buy a house for $80,000 with a $5,000 down payment, and you assume an existing $50,000 loan. The $25,000 balance remaining is carried back by the seller in the form of a purchase-money second mortgage payable under terms you negotiate with the seller. In this particular example, $30,000 represents the seller's equity in the property. You pay $5,000 down, and instead of $25,000 cash, the seller takes back a second mortgage of $25,000.

Terms on the $25,000 purchase-money second are very negotiable and can take shape according to the needs of both the buyer and seller. For instance, probably most advantageous for the buyer would be an interest-only note for a term of ten years. Typically, purchase-money seconds have an interest rate of 10 percent; however this rate is negotiable. Of course, the lower the rate of interest you can negotiate for yourself, the better off you will be financially. I have seen second mortgages retained by sellers as low as 8 percent and as high as 12 percent.

If you do negotiate for an interest-only condition, keep in mind that under an interest-only situation nothing will be applied toward the principal balance owing and the entire principal balance will be due and payable at the end of the term. Although this is definitely a disadvantage, because of inflation you will have the advantage of paying back the entire principal balance of the note at an extended future date with cheaper deflated dollars.

Although interest-only is the least expensive form of note, a fully amortized note payable in equal monthly installments would pay off the entire amount owing by the end of the loan's term. This would inhibit your monthly cash flow because of the higher monthly payment; however the loan would be completely paid off at term's end.

There is a midrange area of negotiation between an interest-only note and a fully amortized note. You could negotiate for a partly amortized note wherein a portion of the principal amount would be paid off monthly; thus you would owe substantially less at the end of the term. Also, you could have a $25,000 balance owing amortized over 20 years and payable in 10 years. This method would keep monthly payments relatively low and would help to pay off a large portion of principal during the 10 years, with only a small balance owing.

Purchase-money seconds are an integral part of profitable real estate investing primarily because you can create inexpensive seller financing which, in most cases, can be assumed by the next buyer. You can actually earn more money by keeping your interest rates low and then reselling your properties at higher rates of interest.

As an example, three years ago I found a great property that, at first glance, appeared impossible to purchase with a small down payment, nor was it likely for the seller to carry back any financing. This beautiful property had an existing 8 percent first loan of $40,000, and the seller wanted $25,000 down. The list price was $119,000, and the listing agent doubted that the seller would be willing to carry back a second loan. Not to be denied, I made an offer of $92,000; I would pay $10,000 down and assume the existing first loan of $40,000, and the seller was to carry back a second loan at 9 percent for the balance owing of $42,000. Neither my agent nor the seller's agent believed this offer had a one-in-a-hundred chance of being accepted. But to everyone's surprise the seller made a counteroffer at a price of $96,000 while accepting all the financing terms of my original offer. Therefore, the only change from my original offer was the price, from $92,000 to $96,000, which increased the amount of the second loan carried back from $42,000 to $46,000. I gladly accepted the counteroffer.

In the above example, I created $46,000 in new low-interest financing on a property that at first glance you'd have thought would never sell under such advantageous terms. Six months after I purchased this lovely money-maker, I sold it for $115,000 on a long-term installment contract, and I would net $350 per month on it for the next 20 years. The main reason for the property's profitability was the low interest rates that were maintained after the sale. I collected 11.5 percent on the total balance owing.

Based on this experience, you never really know whether a seller will carry back a note unless you at least attempt to create low-interest secondary financing by making a legitimate offer.

Take-out Seconds
A "take-out" second loan is different from a purchase-money second loan because it is created from equity in property already owned. For instance, you own a property with $50,000 equity in it. You could take out a second mortgage against that equity to make home improvements, pay for a college education, or buy additional income property. Usually, institutional lenders fund this type of loan in amounts up to 80 percent of the equity in the property. In today's market, take-out seconds cost about 15 percent with loan origination fees of 1 or 2 percent of the amount borrowed.

Take-out seconds are probably the most expensive method of financing real estate and substantially reduce your equity in the property. I would recommend arranging a second loan of this type only when you can use the proceeds to purchase additional income property, and only when that property is an excellent bargain, wherein the investment will at least cover the cost of the new take-out loan.

A special note about second, third, fourth, etc. mortgages. While we are discussing second mortgages, it is important to clear up certain myths or misunderstandings about the safety of these loans. In the 1930s, the era of the Great Depression, many junior lien holders (second, third, etc., mortgage holders) were wiped out in a foreclosure when the borrower did not make loan payments. Back in those days when a first mortgage lender began foreclosure proceedings, the secondary and/or junior lien holders had to pay off the entire first mortgage balance to protect their second mortgage interest and to stop the foreclosure proceedings, otherwise the second mortgage interest would be wiped out in the foreclosure sale.

This is not the case today. Now if the borrower defaults on either a first or second mortgage (or third, fourth, etc.), only the missed payments and late fees, if any, are required to be paid by the secondary lender to protect his mortgage interest. Therefore, in the event of a pending foreclosure by a prior mortgage holder, no longer is the entire balance due in one sum to protect a secondary mortgage.

Equity Sharing

Another method available to finance your purchase is equity sharing, also known as shared equity, equity participation, equity partnership, and shared appreciation. This concept originated out of the need to pair cash-short buyers with cash-rich investors. These two share ownership of the property, and both will gain later when the property is sold for a profit.

Here's how it works. Let's say you are short of cash to make a down payment on a home and your parents want to help. Your parents would agree to make the down payment in exchange for a one-half interest in the house. You agree to occupy the house, maintain it, and pay fair market rent to your parents for their interest in the property. You and your parents split the costs of principal and interest, property taxes, and insurance. Your half-owner parents, because they are rental property owners, can claim income-tax deductions of mortgage interest, property taxes, and depreciation. (If, on the other hand, the parents had made the down payment in the form of a gift, they would receive no tax or appreciation benefits.) Your tax deductions will be the same as for all homeowners, that of mortgage interest and property taxes.

Taking title to a property under equity sharing is the same as purchasing a home on your own. Both parties go on the title according to local statutes, and both parties sign the mortgage note and take responsibility for its payment.

Equity-sharing transactions require one additional step to home ownership. A contract (written agreement) between co-owners is necessary to spell out exactly the important points of the agreement, such as ownership percentages, rent to be charged, buy-out options, specifics on resale, and responsibility for repairs and maintenance. In addition, the contract should specify procedures in the event of death, default, disability, bankruptcy of a co-owner, or acts of God, such as floods, earthquakes, and tornadoes.

Equity sharing then can be beneficial to both the investor and the owner/occupant. The owner/occupant can eventually buy out the investor, sell the house, and use the proceeds for a down payment on another house. The investor has tax advantages from his ownership interest of a rental property and can share in the appreciation.

Chattel Loans

This type of loan is made on the basis of personal property as security for the loan, rather than real property. Automobiles, business equipment, and boats normally qualify for security against a chattel loan. Traditionally these loans are funded for a short term and the cost can be as high as 5 points more than permanent financing, primarily because the security for the loan is so movable, as opposed to real property which is not.

Personal Loans

These loans are made on the basis of your credit-worthiness without security. If you have good credit, you can usually borrow from $5,000 up to $20,000 for a term of up to five years. Your signature alone is all that is required. If you're fortunate enough to qualify for such a loan, it would be advisable for you to do so. This type of funding is ideal for purchasing additional income properties.

FINANCING IN GENERAL

It is a general rule of thumb among lending institutions that "the higher the risk, the higher the interest rate." Since second mortgages are riskier than first mortgages, and likewise developmental financing is riskier than permanent financing, they will carry a higher rate of interest to compensate the lender for the additional risk.

The following material analyzes a question you will likely be faced with in the future: Should you refinance your existing home or take our a second loan? In addition, permanent financing, construction, and development financing will be discussed.

Permanent Financing

First and second mortgages and trust deeds are the most common instruments of real estate financing, and are considered permanent financing. In addition, because of inflation and increased property values, many property owners refinance an existing loan, or loans, already recorded against the property. They can use the tax-free proceeds to invest in additional income properties, or for many other uses.

A good question should now be presented: *Should you refinance or take out a second loan?* Usually homeowners are confronted with this question after they've owned their home several years and would like to spend some of that equity that has accumulated over the years. In most cases, the existing mortgage will be at an interest rate far below the current prevailing rate for new home mortgage loans. If this is the case, then it would be unwise to refinance because you would be eliminating the value of the existing low-interest rate loan by replacing it with a costlier, high-interest rate loan. However, it would be wise to refinance if the prevailing market interest rate for mortgages is 2 points or more below that rate which a person is already paying on the first mortgage. Usually 2 points or more are required to overcome the costs of initiating a new loan, such as loan fees, points, and early payoff penalties.

Instead of refinancing, you also have the option of taking out a second mortgage in order to maintain the value of the existing low rate of interest on the first loan. Let us use, for example, a home purchased six years ago for $50,000 with a first mortgage attached at 8 percent interest for a term of 30 years. The principal and interest payment would be $300 a month. The remaining balance after six years would be approximately $38,000. Since the current market value of the home is $80,000, you therefore have approximately $42,000 equity in the home.

If you refinanced the home at an 11.5 percent rate of interest, the lender would advance 80 percent of the market value, of which $38,000 must be applied toward paying off the balance of the original loan. Thus, there would be $26,000 in net proceeds ($80,000 × 80% = $64,000 − $38,000 = $26,000). The new first loan would require monthly payments of $634 to amortize principal and interest over the 30-year term.

If you arranged a second mortgage for an amount equal to that of refinancing, which is $26,000, in today's market the lender would charge you 13.5 percent for a maximum term of 15 years, which would mean a monthly payment of $338. The total monthly payments of both first and second loans for the next 15 years would be $668 ($338 + $300). After 15 years the second loan would be paid in full, then only a monthly payment of $300 on the existing first loan would be required.

The following tables compare taking out a second loan with refinancing.

As you can see, the difference in amounts paid over the entire term of the loan is a substantial savings of $77,400 when taking out a second mortgage instead of refinancing. When the property is refinanced at 3.5 points above the rate of the existing loan, $38,000 went to pay off the original principal amount, which made for the huge differen-

REFINANCING

Amount of net proceeds	Payment on 1st loan	Term of loan	Total amount paid over term of loan
$26,000	$634	30 yrs	$228,240

TAKING OUT A SECOND MORTGAGE

Amount of net proceeds	Payment on 1st	Term remaining on 1st	Payment on 2nd	Term remaining on 2nd	Total amount paid over term
$26,000	$300	25 yrs.	$338	15 yrs.	$150,840

tial in savings. In addition, although the new second loan interest rate appears high at 13.5 percent, the term is short at 15 years, meaning a substantial savings in the amount of interest that will be paid as the result of the short term of the loan.

Interim or Construction Financing

Construction loans are made on a short-term basis, usually one year, and are used to fund the construction of a new building. Security for the loan is in the underlying land plus the increasing value of the improvement under construction. Periodic installments of the loan proceeds are paid out directly to the contractor or the material suppliers. Once the building is completed, permanent financing is then arranged for a long term to pay off the existing construction loan.

Owing to such risks as cost overruns, mechanic liens, and strikes, construction financing usually costs two to three more points in rate of interest than permanent financing.

Development Financing

This type of funding is common when residential home builders buy a large tract of land, then build homes in phases, selling off each phase as it is completed. A mortgage is used to finance the entire tract and then the lender releases individual parcels from the loan as they are sold off.

Similar to construction financing, development financing is also expensive because of the additional risk realized by the lender.

SOURCES OF REAL ESTATE FINANCING

It definitely pays to shop around when you need financing. If you can save just one point on long-term financing, you will actually save thousands of dollars. And today, more than ever before, there is an abundance of real estate funding available.

Existing Property Sellers

In the existing home sale market the best and least expensive source of funding is the seller, especially the motivated seller. Motivated sellers are ones who will do almost anything to stimulate the sale of their property. This includes accepting a note for the equity in their home at terms that are very advantageous for the buyer. Even without a motivated seller, one can usually acquire a second loan at rates and terms far better than one could from a conventional lender.

A new loan from a conventional lender would typically require credit qualification at a cost of $100, an appraisal report at $150, a loan origination fee of 1 or 2 percent of the loan proceeds, an interest rate at prevailing market interest rates, and, finally, a loan which will not be assumable to another buyer.

Seller financing requires none of these conventional costs, and you can usually negotiate a reasonable rate of interest significantly below market rates. Furthermore, seller financing can be structured to be fully assumable, which is the biggest advantage of all. More on seller financing will be discussed later, but for now it is important that you remember that it is by far your best source of real estate funding.

Savings and Loan Associations

Savings and Loans (S&Ls) are the primary source of new permanent financing of residential real estate. They make conventional loans as well as loans under VA and FHA programs. Typically they lend 80 percent of the value of the home, and will go as high as 95 percent when the borrower is willing to pay for the additional cost of private mortgage insurance. Under terms of refinancing, S&Ls tend to be more conservative and will usually lend only 75 percent of the home's value. Their loan portfolio usually consists of 85 percent residential loans, although they are allowed a limited amount of commercial mortgage loans.

Commercial Banks

Banks are the major source of short-term funding, such as installment loans on vehicles and credit card accounts. Their real estate lending is usually rather limited; however when they do originate home loans, they will usually sell them to other lenders and retain servicing, for which they earn a fee. They are not, however, an outstanding source of home loans, both because of the long-term nature of permanent financing on residential real estate and since commercial banks prefer short-term financing.

Credit Unions

Credit unions are an excellent source of take-out second mortgage loans, and personal or installment vehicle loans. They usually do not fund permanent financing. Credit unions often are partially owned by their shareholders and can operate on thin margins of profit, which allows them to offer more liberal terms than conventional lenders. If you have the opportunity to belong to one, by all means do so. They can be an excellent source both for short-term funding and for some intermediate secured real estate loans as well.

Insurance Companies

Insurance companies are primarily involved with large-scale commercial lending, such as urban shopping centers and high-rise office buildings. They tend to require a higher yield than what residential permanent financing can offer. To generate these higher yields, they often require equity participation, also referred to as an "equity kicker," wherein they can earn a share of the project's gross or net income as well as earning interest on the funded money. Typically, a small portion of their investment portfolio will encompass the purchase of a large package of home loans, whereas a bank or S&L will service the entire loan package.

Syndication of Limited Partnerships

Another method of financing real estate, especially when the investment is beyond your own financial ability, is to form a partnership with other investors. You would be surprised how many potential investors there are who have the money but do not have the time nor the ability to invest on their own. Ideal prospects are those who can better use their time working at their profession, such as doctors, dentists, and lawyers, rather than locating and renting out property.

Successful partnerships begin with the understanding that the limited partners (investors only) will be consulted only on major decisions, such as selling or refinancing the property, and the general partner is responsible for managing the property. Investors should only invest in such partnerships when they will not need their investment capital for the specified number of years of the duration of the partnership. Additionally, buy-out options of each partner's share are also recommended to assist in the survival of the overall partnership.

Before starting any partnership, consult with a trusted attorney to get assistance on drafting all documents. And if you plan to invest as a limited partner, look into the general partner's past experience to arrive at some indication of the potential results.

Loan Brokers

Loan brokers will usually represent pension or trust funds, insurance companies, and some S&Ls. They work independently; however they can represent one or all of the above lenders and charge a fee of 2 points or more for their services. Not only do brokers serve lenders as a medium of investment, they also provide a number of services for their protection. They investigate and appraise the property involved, create and record loan documents, and set up the mechanics for making the transaction convenient. At the option of the lender, they may also assist in making collections.

THE SECONDARY MORTGAGE MARKET

Besides the primary mortgage market, which is the interaction of the borrower with the original lender, there also exists a secondary mortgage market which gives liquidity and flexibility to the overall mortgage lending system. When a lender takes over a loan he himself did not originate, he is engaging in secondary mortgage market activity.

Operatives in the secondary mortgage market will buy lenders' mortgages, thus supplying them with needed cash to originate new loans. Before the emergence of the secondary mortgage market, lenders were often faced with problems regarding liquidity. For example, suppose a long-term lender originates a 30-year mortgage. Although the lender will ultimately recover the principal and earn a substantial amount of interest on the transaction, for 30 years he will have tied up a portion of his assets. These assets, which otherwise might have been available for other, possibly more lucrative, investments are in effect frozen. Finally, if the same lender invests all his assets in mortgages having similar durations, he most definitely will find himself in an illiquid position.

Thus, the dilemma of liquidity is overcome by the buying and selling of loans in the secondary mortgage market. The following are the principal operatives in the secondary mortgage market:

- Federal National Mortgage Association
- Government National Mortgage Association

- Federal Home Loan Mortgage Corporation
- Mortgage Guaranty Insurance Corporation

Federal National Mortgage Association

The FNMA, referred to as "Fannie Mae," originated in 1938 for the purpose of buying and selling government-insured mortgages to assist originators of these loans in liquidating their portfolios. These acquisitions of mortgages are funded by selling notes and debentures.

FNMA buys only certain mortgages of FHA/VA origination that have been funded under strict guidelines. Also the FNMA requires that all sellers purchase FNMA stock.

FNMA conducts biweekly auctions in order to buy mortgages. Prior to the auction the FNMA announces how much money it has available and then commits itself to making certain purchases. The FNMA bases the amount of buying and selling it does on the nation's overall economic climate. During times of tight money when available mortgage money is in short supply, FNMA will buy. In times of loose money, the FNMA sells to investors. This so-called reverse market policy helps to stabilize the overall secondary mortgage market.

Government National Mortgage Association

Founded in 1968, the Government National Mortgage Association, referred to as "Ginnie Mae," is administered by the Department of Housing and Urban Development. Created to take over certain programs phased out of FNMA, the GNMA is authorized to do the following: manage and liquidate the FNMA loan portfolio; operate federally funded housing; oversee high-risk mortgage financing programs and the sale and purchase of government-backed securities.

The GNMA also participates with private lenders in the purchase of large blocks of loan commitments. Then, portions of these loan commitments are sold as securities to the public, backed by a guarantee of the United States Treasury.

Federal Home Loan Mortgage Corporation

The Federal Home Loan Mortgage Corporation, referred to as "Freddie Mac," was founded in 1971. Similar to the other operatives, it functions for the purpose of allowing savings and loans to maintain liquidity for their mortgage assets. The FHLMC buys mortgages from these institutional lenders, supplying them with cash to originate new loans. And, similar to the FNMA, Freddie Mac is funded by selling securities on the open market.

Mortgage Guaranty Insurance Corporation

Also referred to as "Maggie Mae," the Mortgage Guaranty Insurance Corporation, is a private entity specializing in the buying and selling of mortgages and is financed by private funding.

POINTS TO REMEMBER

Proper financing is one of the primary keys to unlocking the door to profitable real estate investing. Low-interest assumable financing allows you so much more flexibility and profit over other methods. If the opportunity is there, remember to try and create seller financing structured to your requirements. If it is necessary to create new financing, be sure and shop around for the best loan, because it is likely you will have to live with this loan for 20 years or more. Just the savings of one point in rate of interest can save you thousands of dollars over the term of the loan. Also try to avoid ARMs and the associated risk these fluctuating loans present.

Furthermore, when you're in the process of negotiating a purchase-money second loan from the seller, try and get the best terms you possibly can. Be sure that the second loan you arrange is fully assumable without a due-on-sale clause so as to allow you more flexibility when you eventually sell the property.

In conclusion, remember the concept of leverage: that the amount invested in the property is relative to the amount of yield, or return you receive on your investment. Always attempt to get the most leverage by keeping your down payment to a minimum. Using OPM (other people's money) to finance your investments will always benefit the borrower (owner) more, especially when the effects of inflation and appreciation are continually increasing the value of the investment.

3 APPRAISAL: A CRASH COURSE AT EVALUATING PROPERTY

To be successful at investing in real estate, it is essential for you to evaluate potential investments accurately. You have to know how to recognize a bargain when you see it, determine how much it will cost to renovate, then determine how much you can honestly sell it for. Determining value, then, is the nuts and bolts of investing in real estate. Without proper appraisal techniques you could be faced with the primary pitfall of real estate investment . . . that of paying too much for investment property.

But you can easily overcome this pitfall by learning the local market. Once you know market values in your particular area and are fully informed of what properties are selling for, you can then be more efficient at locating, and purchasing, a good investment.

The best way for you to learn how to evaluate properties is to review the appraisal methods the professionals use. The following material will assist you at making accurate appraisals on your own and reducing the risk of over-paying when you buy.

APPRAISAL DEFINED

An appraisal of real property is an opinion, or estimate, of a property's value, arrived at by gathering and analyzing pertinent data as of a specific date. The appraisal is based upon the highest and best use of the subject property, the use that will produce the greatest net return. Such an evaluation must take into consideration zoning laws, government regulations, and the overall demand for that type of property in that area.

Appraisal of real property is an art, not a science; the appraiser is actually arriving at a range of values within which the subject property may be expected to sell. Although three different appraisers are likely to arrive at three different opinions of value for a particular property, the figures will probably not be wildly discrepant.

METHODS OF APPRAISAL

Professional appraisers use three methods of appraisal to arrive at a range of value. These methods are *Market Data* or *Comparable Sales Approach*, the *Reproduction Cost Method*, and the *Capitalization Method*. The final opinion of value on a given subject property is determined by weighing the values from each method to arrive at a range of value.

Market Data Method

The market data method, also referred to as the comparable sales method, is the most common method of appraisal used today. This method compares the subject property with similar comparable properties recently sold in the same area. The valuation of the subject property is adjusted up or down according to certain amenities, such as quality of construction, square-footage differential, garage or pool, and individual location.

A simple application of the market data method would be to compare the subject property with three similar properties that have recently sold, are located within the same area, and essentially have no meaningful differences. For instance, assume all three comparables sold at a price between $80,000 and $82,000, and had the same square footage and lot size. The subject property is similar in quality of construction and lot size; however, it has a 300-square-foot den and a swimming pool, which the comparables do not have. Therefore, based on this information, the subject property is worth $81,000, plus the additional amenities of a den and swimming pool. You determine that at today's construction costs a 300-square foot den would cost $40 per square foot, for a total cost of $12,000. You also determine that a swimming pool would cost $10,000. So your final opinion of value would be $81,000 + $12,000 for the den + $10,000 for the pool, or an appraised value of $103,000.

This method of appraisal is used primarily for evaluating single-family residences and condominiums where a number of similar properties are available for comparison.

Reproduction Cost Method

This method is primarily used for the evaluation of certain unique properties, such as public buildings, hospitals, and custom homes. The reproduction cost approach is more appropriate for newer buildings in which depreciation is a minor factor in the overall appraisal.

The reproduction cost method, also referred to as replacement cost

- determines today's cost of replacing all improvements on the property;
- deducts a depreciation allowance to determine the current appraised value of the improvements;
- adds the current appraised value of the improvements to the value of the land.

For example, let's assume the subject property is a ten-year-old custom home on a half acre. It has 2,000 square feet of living space, plus a 400-square-foot garage. Additional amenities include a sprinkler system and a swimming pool.

A simple replacement cost evaluation would be as follows:

First, determine today's value of all the improvements. Today's cost of constructing a new custom home is $50 per square foot, plus $16 per square foot to build a garage. Also, you have to add in the cost of the pool and the sprinkler system.

2,000 square feet × $50	$100,000
400 square feet (garage) × $16	6,400
Cost of pool	10,000
Cost of sprinkler system	600
Total cost of improvements	$117,000
Deduct a depreciation allowance for wear and tear since the property is 10 years old (10% of $117,000)	11,700
Total cost less depreciation	$105,300

Now you have to add in the cost of the land. If comparable vacant half-acre lots in that area are selling for $40,000, then you can add this figure to arrive at a final opinion of value of $145,300.

Note that if the subject property required certain items to be replaced or repaired, those costs would also be reflected in the depreciation allowance.

Capitalization Method

The capitalization method, also referred to as the income approach to appraisal, is primarily used to determine value of income property. It uses the net operating income (NOI) of the subject property, which is then "capitalized" to arrive at fair market value.

To determine NOI, first calculate the gross income of the property at 100 percent occupancy, then deduct for all operating expenses including allowances for bad debts and vacancies. Now the resulting NOI has to be capitalized to arrive at fair market value.

The rate of return upon invested capital is called "capitalization," or "cap rate." It is defined as the rate of return—expressed as a percentage—that is considered reasonable to expect for an investment. The appraiser arbitrarily determines a rate of return, or cap rate, between 8 and 12 percent that must be adjusted based upon the going rate for that type of property. The appraiser determines the cap rate within the 8 to 12 percent range by considering the risk of investment along with the type of property and the quality of the income.

For example, if an investor were considering investing in a high-risk area (high-crime slum area), he would expect a higher rate of return on his investment. Therefore a cap rate of 12 percent would be selected. If the same investor were considering investing in a low-risk prime area of town, he would expect a lower rate of return on his investment, especially since there would be more appreciation in the prime area. Thus, an 8 percent cap rate would be selected. For an in-between area (average), a 10 percent cap rate would be chosen.

The following are two sample forms regarding income and expense information which will assist you at appraising under the capitalization method:

INCOME-PROPERTY STATEMENT

Description: 18- unit apartment building (9 1br, 9 2br)

9 1br at $400 per month rent	$3,600
9 2br at $500 per month rent	4,500
Gross monthly rent	8,100
Net laundry income (rented equipment)	180
Gross monthly income.....................	8,280
Annual gross income	$99,360

1.	Gross annual rental income ($8100 × 12)	$97,200
2.	Other income (laundry $180 × 12)	2,160

3.	Less vacancy and credit loss (5%) $4860	
	Less annual operating expenses	
4.	Trash removal	240
5.	Taxes	13,960
6.	Insurance	3,800
7.	Utilities	4,220
8.	Business license	35
9.	Advertising	360
10.	Resident manager	6,000
11.	Reserve for replacement	4,860
12.	Supplies	240

13.	Total operating expenses incl.		
	vacancy & credit losses 38,575		−38,575
14.	Net operating income		60,785
15.	Loan payments (P & I)		−48,000
16.	Gross spendable income (cash flow)		12,785
17.	plus: Principal payment (equity build up)		+ 3,600
18.	Gross equity income		16,385
19.	less: Depreciation		−17,455
20.	Real estate taxable income		$(1,070)

The following defines each numbered item listed above to assist you at understanding the income-property statement:

1. *Gross annual rental income.* The total annual rent the property would receive at 100 percent occupancy.

2. *Other income.* This item is reserved for additional income other than rent.

3. *Vacancy and credit losses.* Established by the going rate for similar properties in the neighborhood. The national average is 5 percent, with good areas being about 3 percent, and bad as high as 10 percent.

4. *Trash removal.* The total annual cost to remove trash from the property.

5. *Taxes.* Actual real property taxes for the current fiscal year.

6. *Insurance.* This is the total amount for all necessary forms of insurance. If the insurance is part of blanket coverage for several properties, then you must allocate that expense for each separate property.

7. *Utilities.* A figure for a full year's operation, including gas, water, and electricity.

8. *Business license.* Certain cities require a business license to operate apartment buildings. Use the actual cost for the entire year of operation.

9. *Advertising.* This includes the total annual cost of classified advertising and the cost of signs on the property.

10. *Resident manager.* The total cost of the resident manager goes under this item. If you use the service of a management company, that cost can also be included under this item.

11. *Reserve for replacement.* This item covers a reserve fund for all repairs and replacement. These include furniture, drapes, carpet, and all major equipment (elevators, water heaters, pool equipment, etc.). A fair estimate is 5 percent of gross annual rental income.

12. *Supplies.* Rent forms, cleaning supplies, and all miscellaneous items are included in this category.

13. *Total operating expenses.* A summation of all operating expenses before loan payments. As a rule of thumb, annual operating expenses as a percentage of gross annual income should be in a range of from 37 percent to 51 percent, with 40 percent being average.

14. *Net operating income.* The result of deducting total operating expenses from gross annual income. This figure represents what the property would earn if purchased for cash, free and clear of any loans. This item is also used to determine a capitalized value by dividing a suitable cap rate into the net operating income.

15. *Loan payments.* This figure includes principal and interest. The principal portion of the payment is added in under item 17.

16. *Gross spendable income.* The result of deducting annual debt service from NOI, or the actual cash (cash flow) you'll have left over after expenses and debt service.

17. *Principal payment.* This is equity build-up, or that portion of the loan payment which applies toward principal pay off of the loan.

18. *Gross equity income.* The result of adding annual equity payments to the gross spendable income.

19. *Depreciation.* As a general rule, 80 percent of the property's cost can be depreciated for income tax purposes; the remaining 20 percent is allocated to the land, which cannot be depreciated. In this example, cost of the property was $600,000, of which $480,000 could be depreciated for 27.5 years. The result is $17,455 as a depreciation deduction.

20. *Real estate taxable income.* The result of deducting deprecia-tion from gross equity income. Note that although the property gener-ated in excess of $16,000 in income, it actually showed a taxable loss; thus the tax shelter benefit of owning income-producing real estate.

The income-property statement is very important because the numbers it reveals predict how much you're going to make. Normally, the total operating expenses are in a range of 37 percent to 51 percent. Newer buildings fall within the lower range, while older buildings are in the higher range owing to higher maintenance costs.

The net operating income (NOI) is also important, because this is the number which will be capitalized in order to determine appraised value. Now we can use the second form, income-and-expense analy-sis, to determine appraised value using the capitalization method of appraisal.

INCOME-AND-EXPENSE ANALYSIS

Description: 18-unit apartment building
9 1br at $400 per month
9 2br at $500 per month

Gross annual rental income		$ 97,200
Net annual laundry income		2,160
Less: Operating expenses		
Vacancy and credit losses	$ 4,860	
Other operating expenses	33,715	
Total operating expenses		38,575
Net operating income (NOI)		60,785
Capitalization: anticipated rate of return: 10%		
Capitalized value of land and building (divide 10% cap rate into NOI)		607,850
Appraised value using the capitalization method and a cap rate of 10%		$607,850

Now we have determined that an estimate of fair market value based on a 10 percent cap rate is $607,850. We used this rate because the location and quality of the property is average. Now take notice of what happens to the appraised value when different cap rates are applied to the same NOI.

If we apply a cap rate of 8 percent to the same NOI, the following results: $60,785 ÷ 8% = $759,813. And if we apply a cap rate of 12 percent to the same NOI, we see the following: $60,785 ÷ 12% = $506,542.

In conclusion, note the substantial difference in appraised values using different cap rates ($759,813 versus $506,542). In other words, for an investor to earn an 8 percent return using the above NOI, he would have to pay $759,813 for the property; to earn 12 percent, he would have to pay $506,542.

Gross-Income Multiplier Method

This method of determining value cannot be classed as a professional approach to appraisal, yet brokers and investors often use it as a quick off-the-cuff calculation to see whether or not a property deserves further attention. The gross-income multiplier only offers a ballpark estimate. It does not reflect net income or expenses, nor is it reliable in determining true value.

You'll often see newspaper advertisements regarding income property stating "8 times gross" or "5.7 times gross." This means the sales price of that particular property is 8 times or 5.7 times the gross income (i.e., income before deductions for expenses). For example, if gross income is $30,000, then the selling price would be $240,000 at 8 times gross, or $171,000 at 5.7 times gross.

Similar to the capitalization rate, the gross-income multiplier is determined by the appraiser within a range of values considering the going rate for the area. This going rate is normally between 4 and 12, the lower number being for the less-desirable locations.

If the gross income equals $30,000 per year, you have the following valuations using different multipliers:

	Multiplier	Value
Worst area	4	$120,000
Average area	7	210,000
Best area	12	360,000

Now that you're familiar with the appraisal techniques the pros use, it's time to make some important conclusions.

APPRAISAL CONCLUSIONS

The number one priority in making an accurate appraisal is to know the market where you plan to invest. It is not only important to know the prices properties have sold for, but you should also be informed of asking prices. Without adequately knowing the market, it will be impossible for you to accurately determine value. Therefore, to become knowledgeable on local real estate values, start by doing your homework. Obtain a Multiple Listing Service (MLS) book from your friendly agent and get a feel of what's available, and at what price, in your area. Look up recent sales in the back of the MLS book, and especially take note of the price per square foot.

The price per square foot is the most important factor in quickly determining value of improved property. From your research of the MLS book, determine the range that property in your area sells for at price per square foot. From this information alone, you can usually determine whether a property deserves further attention. For example, if you already know that you can sell a particular home at $50 per square foot, then you can be assured that if you buy it at $40 per square foot or less, you will have definitely made a good buy.

Besides the MLS book, you can also become familiar with local values by checking out open houses on weekends. Reading through the local real estate want ads is also helpful at becoming familiar with the local market.

The greatest risk of investing in real estate is paying too much for it. You can avoid this inherent pitfall by carefully analyzing the market before you buy. Well-informed investors know a good buy when they see one and, conversely, are fully aware if a property is overpriced.

A SPECIAL NOTE OF INTEREST

Instead of relying on information from the listing, the broker, or the seller, there are a number of ways you can determine the age of the subject property. Usually inscribed on the inside top of the water closet cover (toilet) you'll note a particular date. This represents the date of manufacture of the water closet, which, give or take six months, corresponds to the date of construction of the building. (However, this date would become unreliable if that particular bathroom had been added to the building at a later date.) Another method of determining age is to check the installation date engraved on the electric or gas meter. And, finally, the Market Analysis Form is useful in evaluating comparable properties and related information.

Market Analysis Form

Subject property adddress _____

Date _____

Information on similar properties in same general area that may have the same approximate value.

Currently for sale

Address	Bedrooms	Baths	Den Fam. rm	Sq. Ft.	Price/ sq. ft.	Mortgages	Interest rate	Days on market

Sold within last six months

Note: Realtors and old MLS books can be helpful for finding past sale information.

4 INVESTING IN REAL ESTATE

Real estate investment will be discussed in three segments: What to look for . . . where to find it . . . and what to do with it once you've got it. However, before these segments can be discussed, it is only fitting that a proper description of such a superior investment be brought forth.

LAND

Before there was anything else . . . there was land. It has, and always has had, certain characteristics typical of nothing else in value. Land has supreme value because unlike anything else, it cannot be increased in quantity. Land is required for the production of food and commodities and provides the location to shelter its landlords and tenants. Land provides natural resources, which in turn are valuable in themselves as oil and mineral products.

Each plot of land is absolutely different from every other plot of land. Each plot has its own soil quality and underlying composition, its own water supply and drainage ability, its own vegetation and terrain, and its own view. With the exception of acts of God, land by itself, unlike the improvements built upon it, cannot be increased in quantity. From feudal kings and landlords of the past to the home-owners and developers of today, a measure of one's wealth has been described primarily in the amount of land one owns. Holding title to land is something precious indeed.

WHAT TO LOOK FOR

The best opportunities available today, especially for the beginner in real estate, are in fix-up properties, since you create value by fixing up run-down properties. You want to buy at a good price from motivated sellers. Furthermore, you want to keep your initial investment in the property to a minimum, thus allowing you more leverage and realizing a greater return on your investment. And, finally, you want to assume low interest rate loans to allow you more profitability and flexibility when you later sell. A good buy forms the foundation for rewarding dividends for years to come.

INGREDIENTS OF A GOOD BUY

In short, the ingredients of a good buy are:

1. Buy at a good price from motivated sellers.
2. Buy only fixer-uppers in which you can create sweat equity.
3. Assume low interest rate loans.
4. Buy with as little down as possible.

Buy at a Good Price from Motivated Sellers
The top priority at successful realty investing is to buy right to sell right. Common sense tells you that before you can sell the property at the right price, you will be required to buy it at the right price . . . and the best buys come from motivated sellers.

What is a motivated seller? A motivated seller (sometimes referred to as a "don't wanter") is someone who because of certain circumstances is prepared to sell below market value. Such circumstances might be: divorce, death in the family, job relocation, vacant rental and associated landlord headaches, lack of money, another property bought and ready to move to. And you might have any combination of the above factors contributing to motivation to sell.

The greatest motivated sellers are those with a combination of the above items, such as lack of money, are currently experiencing vacancies and associated landlord nuisances, or their property has been up for sale for an extended period without any takers. In such situations, the seller would be extremely motivated and prepared to look at just about any offer.

Buy Only Fixer-Uppers
Fixer-uppers come in all shapes and sizes and degree of work required to renovate the entire property. The ideal candidate would be a single family residence (SFR) that just requires cleaning up and a cosmetic paint job inside and out. Less ideal would be a similar house

but one needing substantially more capital and work than simply a paint job, such as new carpeting, roof repair, new kitchen and bathroom tile. More time and cost would be required on the second house, making it less attractive to buy.

But the amount of work required to renovate doesn't matter (as long as the building is structurally sound) if you're not on a limited budget. You can always profit on a fixer-upper as long as the value of the improvement equals twice the cost of such improvement and as long as you bought the property at a bargain price. If you have a limited budget, stick to investing in properties that require minimal amounts to renovate them.

The general rule of thumb for evaluating whether a property is worth fixing up is that every dollar invested in renovation should yield at least two dollars in increased property value (the two for one rule). For example, you buy a home and spend a total of $4,000 renovating it. You should therefore be able to realize at least $8,000 in gain after a sale.

Properties become run down primarily owing to lack of care and adequate maintenance. Often the landscaping is overgrown, trash is strewn about inside and out. The place probably stinks to high heaven, while even a few windows are found to be broken. This shabby and unhealthy condition presents a great opportunity for the shrewd investor. All this described filth and destruction substantially lowers the value of this home. All you have to do is determine what it will cost to clean and renovate this home and the price for which you can reasonably sell it and earn a profit.

Assume Low-Interest Rate Loans

I cannot begin to impress upon you the importance of assuming low interest rate loans. The advantages of this method of financing are gigantic when compared with other common methods of financing, and yet critical to the amount of potential success you'll have at investing.

First, a definition is in order. Low-interest rates are considered to be anything at 10 percent or less. Avoid interest rates in excess of 10 percent. Assumable loans are, in most cases, existing VA and FHA loans originated by previous or existing sellers. (Note that on rare occasions some conventional loans can be assumed. Furthermore, certain FHA loans originated after January 1, 1987, cannot be assumed until two years have elapsed from date of loan origination.)

Assumable loans do not require credit qualification (in other words, no questions are asked), and the assumptor is only charged a minimal assumption fee (usually $50). Furthermore, an assumable loan can be assumed by the subsequent buyer, which means you have built-in financing on the property. Finally, the ease and simplicity of loan assumption allows you to close a real estate purchase within 10 days, as opposed to 60 to 120 days under other common methods of financing.

Let's compare low interest rate loan assumption with other methods of financing. First look at the comparable costs. Under loan assumption a small $50 fee is charged, with no questions asked. Under a conventional loan, you're required to fill out a complicated loan request application form. Then, if your loan is approved, you're required to pay an appraisal fee of about $150, a credit application fee of about $75, and a loan origination fee of 1 to 2 percent of the borrowed amount (e.g., on an $80,000 loan you would have to pay between $800 and $1,600 for a loan origination fee). Finally, a conventional loan would require 30 to 60 days to close, and most likely it would not be assumable by any subsequent buyers.

Comparing low interest rate loan assumption to originating new financing under VA and FHA is not quite as staggering. The differential is minimized because the seller absorbs most of the costs. How-

CONVENTIONAL LOAN

Cost to originate:		
Appraisal	$ 150	
Credit report	75	
Loan-origination fee—2% of loan (80,000)	1,600	
Total	$1,825	
Cost over term of the loan:		
$80,000 loan @ 11% for 30 years (monthly payment of $761.86 [$761.86 × 360 months = $274,270]		
Total payout over term of loan		$274,270
Cost to originate		1,825
Total		$276,095

LOAN ASSUMPTION

Cost to assume	$ 50	
Cost over term of loan ($80,000 loan @ 8% for 30 years = $587.02 per month [$587.02 × 360]		211,327
Total cost over term of loan =		$211,377

ever, the borrower is still required to pay the cost of appraisal and the credit report. In addition, borrowing under VA and FHA methods delays the closing of the transaction 60 to 120 days owing to red tape and the cumbersome tactics of federal agencies.

As you can see, the difference in these methods of financing can be substantial. Under conventional methods, it could cost you almost $2,000 to originate a loan at an interest rate likely to be higher than what you could assume. This means that over the entire term of the loan you could save upwards of $30,000 using loan assumption. See the illustrative example of a conventional loan and loan assumption.

From the above example it can be seen that the cost over the full term of the conventional loan is $276,095, as compared with $211,377 for loan assumption. The difference is $64,718 in savings, and that's not taking into account the other three major advantages of loan assumption: (1) you don't have to qualify for credit; (2) you can often close the transaction within 10 days; (3) you benefit from built-in financing as the subsequent buyer can assume the loan.

Buy with as Little Down as Possible

Remember the importance of leverage and how it affects your return on investment? (Look back at Chapter 3.) The smaller the amount of investment, the greater the amount of yield you will realize on that investment. If you invest too much cash in a down payment, you not only minimize the yield but you also seriously limit your selling options. Excessive down payments require you to recover large amounts of cash through a sale, which inhibits the number of prospective buyers who might be interested in your property.

For example, let's say you have $20,000 in ready cash available for investment. You have the option of investing the entire amount in one property, or you could buy four individual properties ($5,000 each) with this significant amount. Putting the entire amount into one property would limit your future purchasing power because you would have nothing left for further investment. Likewise, your return on investment would be substantially smaller than it would be if you had made a lesser down payment. Also, you would tend to require more of a down payment from a buyer in order to recoup your huge investment, thus inhibiting the property's saleability. Besides, the return on investment and net income would be much greater if $20,000 were better used to purchase four properties, instead of one.

5 SOURCES OF POTENTIAL BARGAINS (Where To Find Them)

Available sources of real estate investment range from scanning the local newspapers and your realtor's multiple listing service to locating HUD properties and seeking out property in distress or that has been foreclosed on.

Up to this point we have discussed what to look for in a real estate investment. Now we will focus on where to find it.

If it was easy to locate and purchase bargain-priced real estate, everyone would be doing so. Since it is not, perseverance is needed to first locate and then buy the right property for you.

NEWSPAPERS

You'll find homes and multi-unit buildings listed in the classified section of your local newspaper under "Real Estate For Sale." Circle with a pen the properties that appear interesting, then cut them out and staple the circled ads to the left-hand margin of a plain piece of paper. Now you have adequate space to make notes adjacent to the stapled-down advertisement.

Begin calling on the cut-out advertisements. Inquire into the available financing and down-payment requirements. Ask about the square footage, lot size, condition of the property, and the reason they are selling. Get as much information as you can. Then, if the property still sounds promising, make an appointment with the owner to visit it.

REALTORS AND MLS

A good real estate agent is a priceless asset. A good agent is looking out for your interest. He or she makes available to you properties that you otherwise would not have access to. When you do locate the property which deserves an offer to purchase, your agent will present the offer, while representing your interest, and will help with negotiating the final agreement between buyer and seller. Then the agent follows the transaction through its normal channels, securing any loose ends that might otherwise jeopardize the final closing.

To work effectively, a good agent needs to know exactly what you're looking for. Give him specific details of exactly what it is you want. For instance, a fixer-upper priced below $100,000, with assumable loans at 10 percent or less, requiring a down payment of $7,000 or less. These are specific parameters that act as guidelines for the agent. A good agent will avoid showing you anything outside these parameters.

A good agent has access to the Multiple Listing Service (MLS), which covers every home listed for sale with a realtor in your area. It's the agent's responsibility to keep abreast of what's on the market and to be looking for property you are interested in. Furthermore, the agent is important to you because he has the key to the lock box that opens the door to all properties listed with the MLS.

Real estate agents who belong to the MLS have available the MLS book, which is usually published every other week, maintaining up-to-date information on all listed properties. It is an invaluable tool to investors. Once you get to know an agent, ask him to lend you last week's MLS book so you can study the listings. (Technically speaking, lending out MLS books to nonmembers is against MLS rules, however it is done all the time.)

Once you have a recent MLS book, carefully go through it while noting properties of interest. On a separate sheet of paper, note the property address and MLS page number. Then, later when you call on, or drive by the property, you can make notes on the reference sheet instead of the MLS book. Also, important information regarding recent sales prices are usually listed in the back portion of the MLS book, and this information will help you to get a feel for values in the local market.

How To Find a Good Agent

You can use several methods to acquire a good agent. Talk to friends and neighbors and ask them if they could refer you to one. Or you could call on several listed properties. Real estate agents typically list properties, then allocate floor time to answer calls on listings with the intention of accumulating a clientele of buyers to work with. Or you could use the unconventional method of walking into a real estate office and observing the surroundings. The more active and successful agents in the office decorate their walls and desk with certain awards and mementos, such as Member of the Million Dollar Club, or Salesman of the Month, and so on. Make a selection and go over and introduce yourself. Tell him exactly what you're looking for, then give him a month or two to get results. If your new agent doesn't come up with a suitable property within that time, do not hesitate to find another.

Personally, I use the services of one agent exclusively for locating listed property, and the services of another for help in negotiating with For Sale By Owners (FSBOs). Jacquay Manos of Americana Group in Las Vegas is my exclusive agent for locating listed property. She was referred to me through a friend and turned out to be the best agent I've ever had. In my opinion, what makes Jacquay a good agent is the work she does before visiting the property. She feeds into the MLS computer exactly what it is I'm looking for, then when the data comes out, she puts each property on a separate 8.5" × 11" sheet of paper. All the data are then stapled together and she highlights in red ink certain information, such as "overpriced" or "poor location." The data that come out of the computer are all listed properties that meet my particular requirements, thereby enabling me to efficiently pick out the ones that deserve further attention.

When I deal with FSBOs, I find it more effective to use an agent to present offers and act as my negotiator. Mike Snyder of Snyder Realty is great at representing my interest and pointing out certain items I may have overlooked. Usually a third-party agent is beneficial to a buyer because the agent can meet directly with the seller and perform certain duties that are often awkward for a buyer. (As when a skilled agent, upon presentation of an offer to purchase, can point out certain deficiencies in the property without offending the seller, thereby substantiating the low price being offered). Furthermore, a skilled agent knows how to point out the benefits to the seller of carrying a note for his equity in the property rather than accepting cash.

OTHER BARGAIN-HUNTING METHODS

In addition to want ads and using a realtor and the MLS, great bargains can be found just by "cruising" the neighborhood. This means selecting a particular neighborhood where you would like to buy property and driving up and down the streets taking notes. This includes noting listed properties as well as FSBOs. While you're at it, keep an eye out for property that appears likely to be for sale. Telltale signs of potential bargains are vacant properties, unattended lawns, and homes that require paint.

Once you've accumulated a substantial list, you can obtain ownership records (usually from your local county courthouse or the property tax collector's office).

Also, consider inserting an advertisement in the local newspaper, such as "Real Estate Wanted." You'll surely receive a few flaky calls, but, you never know, one good bargain could pay for three years of advertising.

In conclusion, how to invest in foreclosures and HUD property, which are additional sources of investing available to you, is detailed in the next two chapters.

6 FORECLOSURES: HOW TO BUY REAL ESTATE IN DISTRESS

Another great source of investment is distressed property, such as property in foreclosure. One of the best buys I ever made was a 19-unit apartment building in foreclosure. Distressed property has always been a popular investment, especially since it is often sold substantially below market value.

Real estate in foreclosure is a specialized market. Frankly, there is a lack of adequate material written about the subject, yet everyone knows about this market. Foreclosure property, then, can be compared with the famous lost Dutchman Mine: everyone is aware of it, but nobody knows where it is.

Fortunately for me, many years ago while I was working as an appraiser for a large savings and loan, I was transferred to the REO department because of my previous property management experience. REO, in case you don't already know, is "Real Estate Owned," which is real property owned by an institutional lender and acquired through foreclosure proceedings.

This particular savings and loan needed all the help it could get in the REO department, because there were numerous bad loans on its books which had gotten there during the time when they became so large (35 branches) by buying out smaller companies. The department eventually had to foreclose on over $4 million worth of real estate, and it was my job to manage and dispose of this property. This inventory consisted of dilapidated single family homes in the midst of riot-torn Watts and 40-unit, rat-infested apartment buildings without windows or parking facilities. Trust me when I say these properties were a landlord's nightmare. But we eventually sold off most of them.

From this experience I would like to make two key points about distressed real estate.

1. If you plan to buy foreclosure property, remember . . . what you see is not always what you get. Property that has been foreclosed on is usually in more disrepair than first meets the eye. It is unlikely that the owner who is delinquent in loan payments has been adequately maintaining the building for several years. The last thing a financially troubled owner does is get behind in loan payments (but the first thing he'll do is defer maintenance), otherwise he knows that the lender will foreclose. Often the maintenance is neglected for years before the actual act of foreclosure occurs.

Therefore, if you happen to be interested in a foreclosed property, estimate the costs to repair the building, then, just to be safe, add another 25 percent to cover you for any unforeseen repairs that are likely to show up after you own the building.

2. Do not, by any means, leave a property unattended for an extended period of time. While I worked for the savings and loan we made sure that the day we took title to a property was the day that that particular property was secured. Regardless of the quality of the neighborhood, we immediately sent out a crew to board up all windows and doors. Without properly securing the property, the following scenario could happen: In one night I have seen an entire house gutted from top to bottom; all the plumbing fixtures, including tubs and sinks, built-ins, anything even of marginal value was ripped right from the wall. Further, a likely target for a stone-throwing delinquent is a glass window pane without a protective board over it. Teenage gangs have been known to make unsecured houses their operational headquarters, and the homeless have also been known to hold up for months in such accommodations.

Finally, when you buy a boarded-up foreclosure, if the property is unattended, keep all the boards up until you finish with the renovation. If you purchase the property unboarded and you plan to renovate it without anyone living there, board it up until it's renovated and you have tenants for it. This way you'll avoid the frustration of witnessing all your renovation destroyed by malicious people.

THE THREE PHASES OF FORECLOSURE

The process of foreclosure goes through three phases, and an investor can purchase the distressed property in any one of these phases.

property owner who defaults (fails to make payments when due) on a loan is notified by the lender that it is initiating legal procedures that will eventually lead to a foreclosure sale.

2. Unless the payments—including late fees and penalties—which are in arrears are made, the property goes up for sale at public auction. The lender who is foreclosing initiates the bidding, usually at the price which represents his interest, including late fees and penalties. The highest bidder pays off the loan (in cash) and claims the property.

3. If the property does not sell at auction, it reverts to the lender, and if that lender happens to be a financial institution, the property then becomes REO.

Purchasing real estate during the first phase of foreclosure can often get you a real bargain. However, the many difficulties associated with such property can often lead you to something you never bargained for. For instance, there may be liens against the property and you may find that, although you were able to purchase the property quite easily, you must also buy it back from the IRS, county tax assessor, or some other entity which has attached a lien to the property. Unless you do exhaustive research before getting involved in a foreclosure property, you could get stuck having valuable working capital tied up waiting for liens against the property to be cleared up or for a title search to be conducted. In the end, your so-called "bargain" may cost a lot more than you had contemplated.

Should a property have problems, you automatically assume them when you purchase it. Property purchased during the first phase of foreclosure requires much research and time, and even then you may end up with your funds tied up in escrow for an extended period.

When you purchase property in the second phase—at public auction—you're faced with similar problems, and you must thoroughly investigate the property before you bid. Furthermore, let me again remind you that you are required to pay cash for the property.

It is in the third phase—when the institutional lender has title to the property as REO—that the property emerges as an extremely attractive venture for the investor. But before going any further, you should be made aware of an institutional lender's attitude toward REO: They don't want anything to do with it!

Institutional lenders are in the business to earn money by lending out their funds, and in so doing to earn interest and points. They take in savings deposits then lend these deposits out on long-term real estate loans. Of course, the property itself is used as collateral to secure the loan against the possibility of default by the borrower. Occasionally they are required to foreclose on a property when a loan goes sour. The property is essentially unwanted. The lender would prefer to sell the REO and use the proceeds to fund another loan, therefore, institutional lenders will usually offer attractive terms to an investor to relieve the institution of the unwanted property once it's on the books as REO.

Acquiring Property in the First Phase
Should you decide to invest in distressed property before the actual foreclosure sale, it will be necessary for you to deal directly with troubled owners. The following procedures are required to be successful:

1. Learn the terminology
2. Acquaint yourself with the sources
3. Select a territory in which to operate
4. Prepare a list of potential investments
5. Prepare an investment analysis
6. Meet and negotiate with the owner
7. Estimate the costs
8. Gather all the data
9. Closing the deal.

Now we can examine each procedure in more detail.

Learn the Terminology
Investing in foreclosure property is a specialized business. Some of the terms and phrases associated with it are unique and it is imperative that you learn the proper phraseology and procedures so as to portray yourself to property owners as a knowledgeable person. Thus you will function more efficiently and effectively at acquiring worthwhile properties.

What is foreclosure? It is the procedure where property pledged as security for a debt is sold to pay that debt in the event of default in payment and terms. The process of foreclosure varies from state to state throughout America, but the procedure is similar nationwide. The primary difference is between states that use a mortgage instrument as security and those that use a deed of trust.

Mortgage and Deed of Trust. Mortgages and Trust Deeds (or Deeds of Trust) are written instruments that create liens against real property. Should the borrower default on the loan, these instruments allow the lender to sell the secured property in order to satisfy the loan obligation.

A mortgage instrument involves two parties: one is referred to as the *mortgagor*, who is the borrower or property owner, and the other as the *mortgagee*, who is the lender. A mortgage has two parts: the *mortgage note*, which is evidence of the debt, and the *mortgage contract*, which is security for the debt. The note promises to repay the loan, while the contract promises to convey title of the property to the mortgagee in case of default.

Should the mortgagor fail to make payments, the property can then be sold through foreclosure in a court action. (Note that "court action" is not required under a deed of trust, and this is the primary difference between the two instruments.) To initiate foreclosure proceedings, the mortgagee must first obtain from the court a foreclosure judgment ordering the sheriff to sell the property to the highest bidder (over and above what is due the lender). The property is then put up for sale at public auction.

Once a successful bid is made, the bidder receives from the sheriff a document known as the *certificate of sale*. In most cases, the bidder must then hold the certificate for one year. He then receives a deed to the property if the mortgagor does not pay the outstanding debt. In many states if the mortgagor pays the outstanding debt during this period, he then retains ownership of the property and the foreclosure sale is nullified. The mortgagor's privilege of redeeming the property during this period is referred to as the mortgagor's *equity of redemption*.

A deed of trust is similar to a mortgage instrument except that an additional third party is involved and the foreclosure period (without court action) is much shorter.

Under a deed of trust, the borrower or property owner is called the *trustor*, and the lender is the *beneficiary*. The intermediate party, whose function is to hold title to the property for the security of the lender, is called the *trustee*. Should the trustor default on the loan obligation, the subject property will be sold by the trustee at public auction through a "power-of-sale" clause contained in every deed of trust.

Foreclosure is initiated by a *notice of default*, which is recorded by the trustee, with a copy sent to the trustor. After three months, a *notice of sale* is posted on the property, and an advertisement for sale is carried in local newspapers once a week for three weeks. If during this period the trustor fails to pay the beneficiary sufficient funds to halt the foreclosure (overdue loan payments plus interest, penalties, and late fees), the sale will be conducted by the trustee. Proceeds from the foreclosure sale are disbursed to the beneficiary, then to any other lien holders.

Assignment of Mortgage (or Deed of Trust). A written financial document transferring the rights of the beneficiary (mortgagee) under a mortgage or deed of trust to another party.

Substitution of Trustee. A written document, usually found on the reverse side of a deed of trust, that transfers trusteeship. Transfers, or substitutions of trustees, are made for reasons of convenience or for better personal service. Legally the beneficiary can also be trustee. The purpose of doing so is to gain control of a trustee sale.

Notice of Action (Lis Pendens). The legal term for a notice that a lawsuit is pending on the subject property is *lis pendens* (litigation pending). It gives notice that anyone acquiring interest in the subject property after the date of notice may be bound by the outcome of the pending litigation.

Obviously, you should be concerned when such a notice is attached to a property you're interested in. Unlike most other liens and attachments, a foreclosure sale seldom wipes out this pending litigation.

Recision. The act of nullifying the foreclosure process. It places the property back to its previous condition, before the default from the title records.

Power of Sale. A power-of-sale clause is written into every deed of trust giving the trustee the right to advertise and sell the secured property at public auction should the trustor default on the loan. This clause enables the trustee to sell the secured property without court action. When the sale is completed at the public auction, the trustee will convey title to the purchaser, use the funds from the proceeds to satisfy the beneficiary, then return surplus monies, if any, to the trustor. Once all this is accomplished, the trustor is entirely divested of the property and has no right of redemption.

Acquaint Yourself with the Sources
You have four available sources to tap for property in distress:

1. The REO listing of institutional lenders;
2. Legal newspapers; (in states where such published notice is required);

3. Fee subscription services that publish defaults and foreclosure sale notices; and

4. The county recorder's office, which records notices relevant to foreclosure.

Information regarding real estate in foreclosure is available through the above sources. Services that provide such information vary throughout the country with each state's legal requirements. Some states require that the notice of default be publicized in a legal publication, while many legal newspapers publish such notices routinely as a community service. Further, some companies make available public-record services on a fee-subscription basis. Both the legal publications and the fee-subscription sources obtain their information directly from the county recorder's office. Their published information is rearranged into a less complicated and easier-to-read form. The cost of the convenient fee-subscription service is substantially higher than either that of legal publications or the information available at no cost from the public records or the county recorder.

Of course, you could acquire these data on recorded defaults directly from the county recorder, where this information is recorded daily and is for public use.

Once the default has been recorded and the redemption period has elapsed, the notice of sale is published. But this legal notice cannot be found at the county recorder's office, because the trustee is required only to publish, not to record, this notice. This is where the subscription services, legal newspapers, and local newspapers come into play, for they are authorized to publish such notices. In addition, you'll often see these postings on bulletin boards in your county courthouse.

Keep in mind that services which publish notices of default are not liable for the accuracy of the information. You may find incorrect addresses or other incorrect information published by such services. The only data that can be deemed reliable are the actual recordings found in the county recorder's office.

These published services do not state whether the instrument in default is a first, second, or third mortgage. To determine which of the liens is in default, you'll have to make a personal visit to the county recorder's office and look it up yourself.

Occasionally, these legal notices of default omit the exact street address of the property. If this is the case, the correct address can be obtained by consulting the map books available while you're at the county recorder's office. Match the legal description given with the address in the map books.

After you obtain the required information about a distressed property and you drive by for a personal inspection of it, you'll note an interesting phenomenon. Property in foreclosure, 99 times out of a 100, always has the same appearance. You can literally spot the neglected property a block away. It's the only house on the block with a dried-out, unmowed lawn with debris scattered about. You'll probably notice a broken window or two and it probably requires paint. This neglected house, which once was probably a nice home, stands out in the neighborhood like a sour grapefruit in a crate of fresh red apples.

At one time, the trustee would offer necessary information about the default to the public as a professional courtesy. This service, unfortunately, is no longer given so freely, primarily because of the increasing popularity of investing in foreclosures, which then developed into a nuisance for the trustee. Today the trustee is obligated only to provide information regarding date, time, and location of the sale.

Select a Territory in Which To Operate

To be most effective, restrict your operations to a specific area within your city. An appropriate area is the surrounding neighborhood in which you live. Working within a designated area close to home will make it easier to develop contacts and to ascertain property values. Furthermore, the area you select should have a potential for growth— as opposed to a declining area—which eventually can lead to an increase in property values.

Once you choose the designated territory, begin accumulating information relevant to events occurring in that area. Obtain a large map of the area, then note sales prices of homes, location of schools, and specific streets where resales offer higher value per square foot of house. In addition, note particular areas that show signs of declining value that might be the result of crime, poor land planning, or traffic congestion.

Limit your operational zone to an area not to exceed 2,000 homes. Obtain a large map of the area from the county assessor's or county clerk's office. As trends and events occur, note them on your map in pencil. Include positive or negative trends and events that may have an economic impact on your designated area.

After you gain some experience and are somewhat of a specialist in distressed property, you no longer have to confine your activities to single-family residences. Get to know values of multi-unit buildings, raw acreage, and office or industrial projects.

Prepare a List of Potential Investments

After you're acquainted with the territory and the sources of distressed property, you can then begin to narrow down the total supply of foreclosures from the information compiled. Start with all available Real Estate Owned from your meetings with REO managers. Then compile available property through the sources mentioned earlier (legal publications, subscription services, and the county recorder's office).

Write down all pertinent data on each property on the Property Information Form which is illustrated below. This form lists all the vital information you need to make a financial analysis and close the deal successfully.

Additional potential investments can be developed while you're acquainting yourself with the designated territory. If you're alert, you can often spot signs of property that eventually, if not immediately, will be in distress. Run-down homes with debris scattered about are often rented out by absentee landlords, frequently are abandoned by tenants, and the absentee landlord should be contacted immediately to procure a sale.

Absentee landlords often board up vacated property, especially in declining neighborhoods, to protect doors and windows from vandals. If you spot a boarded-up house which is not already on your list, find out who the owner is and attempt to make a deal.

PROPERTY INFORMATION FORM

Lot # _____ Block # _____
Map page # _____
Owner's name: _____
Property address: _____
Phone: (home) _____ (work) _____
Date default action taken: _____ Final date to correct: _____
First Loan Data
    Lender's name: _____ Loan #: _____
    Type: _____ Is it assumable? _____
    Interest rate: _____ Original principal owing: _____
    Balance as of: _____ is _____
    with monthly payments of _____ and annual taxes of _____

Second Loan Data
    Lender's name: _____ Loan #: _____
    Type: _____ Is it assumable? _____
    Interest rate: _____ Original principal owing: _____
    Balance as of: _____ is _____
    with monthly payments of _____.

Loan payments in arrears:

First loan $ _____ # of months at _____ _____

Second loan $ _____ # of months at _____ _____

Third loan $ _____ # of months at _____ _____

Total late charges   _____

Total default and foreclosure fees   _____

Grand total of amount in arrears as of _____ _____

Description of other liens:

1. _____ as of _____ total owing
   including penalties is _____.

2. _____ as of _____ total owing
   including penalties is _____.

- -

Sq. footage of livable area _____ Lot size _____

# of bedrooms _____ # of baths _____ Dining _____ Garage _____

Estimated cost to repair interior (describe rooms & work required) _____

_____

_____

Total estimated cost of interior and exterior _____

Property location factors (good, average, below average):

Lot _____ Shopping _____ Public transportation _____

Schools _____ Parks and other _____ Freeways _____

Preliminary cost estimates:

Preliminary cost of all delinquencies   _____

Title and escrow expenses   _____

Loan transfer or origination fee   _____

One month's P&I + taxes and insurance   _____

Cash required for additional   _____

Total cash required to make current   _____

Total interior and exterior repair costs   _____

Prepare an Investment Analysis

Now that you have listed potential investments, it's time to prepare a financial analysis of those properties deserving further consideration. From the Property Information Form, you can gather more detailed information and an estimate of what you feel the property is worth after renovation. This will prepare you to contact the troubled owner.

Meet and Negotiate with the Owner

Bear in mind at all times that the purpose of your visit to the property is not only to make a good investment but also to maintain a proper attitude which will aid the troubled owner in his distressed situation. If everything goes according to the plan, the owner will receive cash for some of his equity, his credit will be salvaged, and you will acquire title to the property.

Refrain from phoning the owner until after you have personally met with him. This keeps the owner from giving you the brush-off over the phone. A personal visit is not only more businesslike but also gives you the opportunity of looking over the property.

Begin with a simple introduction of who you are and why you're there, suggesting a mood of mutual assistance. Mention that you have discovered through your sources that the property might be for sale. If in fact the property is for sale, you can immediately get into details of the transaction. However, if the owner does not have the property up for sale, a different approach is required.

Time is important when negotiating to purchase property in foreclosure, since it is on the side of you, the investor. Pressure is on the troubled owner to remedy the situation so as not to lose the property and good-credit rating. It is to your advantage to remind the homeowner that, while you're interested in making a good investment for yourself, it will also be a good decision for him since he can realize some cash and preserve his credit rating.

During these periods of stress faced by homeowners in foreclosure proceedings, it is important to remember that they often disguise the truth about certain matters. Understandably, the loss of home and property is a horrible event. Therefore it's essential that all details about the property be verified.

Should the owner miraculously remedy his troubled financial condition and bring delinquent payments up to date, be happy for him. But at the same time continue to keep in touch, because now the homeowner is faced with an additional problem: how to keep up with the existing house payments, plus paying back the additional funds borrowed to cure the initial crisis. Chances are, if you continue to stay in touch, the opportunity to buy the home will arise once again.

The following are suggested approaches to use in order to stimulate negotiations with an owner in foreclosure:

"If you'll allow me to make a complete financial analysis of the property, I can be back within 24 hours with a firm offer that will solve your current dilemma."

"My purpose in being here is to offer you cash for your equity, which you would lose in a foreclosure sale. Therefore, by working with me you can salvage your credit, drive away much better off, and start all over again."

"Please allow me to see the documents on your home. Do you have the deed, the title policy, and the loan payment record?"

As a professional investor, you can act faster and offer more results to a troubled owner than anyone else. (A real estate agent would require a sizable commission—a needless expense when you purchase the property.)

Do not be concerned with excessive damage to the house as long as it is structurally sound, for a run-down house usually presents more opportunity for the investor. In fact, the more run-down, the better. Every defect offers profitable opportunity to the shrewd distressed property investor.

Each defect must be noted, then an accurate cost estimate be made to correct such defects. Your deal with the owner will then be made on the basis of the estimated repair cost, plus a reasonable profit for you. Once you acquire the property, make every effort to renovate it within the budget arrived at under your repair-cost estimate.

You need not be a jack-of-all-trades and repair everything yourself, but it's essential to be accurate at discovering problems and at knowing how much it will cost to repair each problem. You must know what the renovated home will sell for in that particular neighborhood. It is obviously poor judgment to invest in a property if the total cost of renovation plus purchase price is greater than its market value.

By thoroughly checking out the entire property, carefully analyzing it, then honestly evaluating the sales price once renovation is complete, you can rest assured that the risk has been minimized and a profit will be realized.

If you've analyzed the numbers carefully and the total costs of renovation and acquisition are more than the resale value, don't entirely abandon the project. Go back to the troubled owner and reopen negotiations. Point out that it is necessary for you to make a reasonable profit, but if you're still unable to arrive at a reasonable transaction, then, indeed, it's time to look elsewhere.

Estimate the Costs
The least complicated way to acquire property in foreclosure during the first phase is to assume the existing loan while making up all loan payments in arrears, then purchasing the deed, and finally taking possession of the property. Very neat and clean. But, more often than not, you'll be required to involve yourself with details that tend to complicate matters involving distressed property. To simplify matters, use the Cost-Estimate Form which follows. It considers all the items relevant to investing in foreclosed property.

Purchasing the Deed
Check the *grant deed* or the *title insurance policy* to make certain that the owner has the property vested in his name. If neither of these is

COST-ESTIMATE FORM

Address _____

Cost of acquiring property:
   Purchasing the deed $ _____

   Delinquent taxes   _____

   Bonds and assessments   _____

   Delinquencies on first loan:
   _____ months at $ _____   _____

   Total late charges and fees   _____

   Advances   _____

   Pay off second loan (include all
   delinquencies, advances, and fees)   _____

Preliminary cost estimates:
   Title and escrow expenses   _____

   Loan transfer or origination fee   _____

   1 month P&I + taxes and insurance _____

Total cash to purchase   _____

   Balance of all loans after purchase _____

   Other encumbrances   _____

Total property cost (before repairs) _____

Cost of repairs needed:

Paint _____	Plumbing _____	Roof _____
Electrical _____	Termite _____	Fencing _____
Landscape _____	Floors _____	Carpeting _____
Wallpaper _____	Fixtures _____	Hardware _____

Total cost of repairs   _____

Total property cost (after repairs)   _____

---

available, check the escrow documents from when the owner purchased the property. If none of these is available for verification, check the official records at the county recorder's office.

You must know the difference between a grant deed and a *quit-claim deed*. An owner of real property who issues a grant deed is warranting that he has marketable title to the property. A quit-claim deed simply releases any interest the grantor may have in the property. A grantor who has no interest in the property is not releasing anything. For example, assume you give me a quitclaim deed on the Golden Gate Bridge. If you have no interest whatsoever in the Golden Gate Bridge, you're simply executing a statement saying, "I have no interest whatsoever in the Golden Gate Bridge." Obviously you have no ownership interest in it, and you're releasing nothing. If you accept a quitclaim deed, it's imperative that the grantor have an interest to convey to you.

Real Estate Taxes

Only rarely are delinquent property taxes assessed against a property; occasionally up to three years' worth could have accumulated, as is often the case when the lender fails to provide for an impound account for hazard insurance and property taxes. With an impound account, the borrower pays a prorated share of these expenses monthly into a trust, out of which the lender pays these liabilities.

If you're involved with properties which have VA or FHA loans on them, you can be assured that tax payments are up to date, because these government-backed loans automatically provide for an impound account.

The best method of making sure that property taxes have been paid is to get information directly from the county tax collector. All that is required is a simple phone call to the county tax collector, providing the complete legal description of the property.

Bonds and Assessments

Most frequently, bonds and assessments show up in less than fully developed areas where sewers and sidewalks have not been completed. To fund the construction of sewers and sidewalks, the county will usually assess property owners for the construction of these items and attach a lien to the property until the amount assessed is paid in full. Be very careful of these liens against real property because they do not always appear on the title report. These liens are recorded against real property and are written in a way to allow the homeowner to pay them off monthly over a period of years. However, in some cases, these liens have to be paid in full when the property is sold.

To verify whether any bonds or assessments are outstanding, or to learn any other details about them, call the tax department or the county treasurer.

Existing Loans

Probably the most important consideration in purchasing a property in foreclosure is the existing loans. Because there are a variety of ways the property could have been financed, you should be familiar with all the methods described in Chapter 2 on financing.

VA and FHA loans offer the foreclosure investor much more flexibility than do conventional loans, since they require no credit qualification, and the interest rate cannot be changed. Nor will there be a prepayment penalty if the loan is at least two years old.

If the property you're interested in has a conventional loan, then it is likely the new borrower will have to qualify, and that the interest rate will be adjusted upwards to reflect the market rate. Furthermore, conventional lenders are known to charge a 1 to 2 percent assumption fee on the unpaid balance.

Conventional lenders vary substantially in their methods of handling delinquencies. However, they're normally stricter than government-backed loans on the matter of allowing a borrower in a conventional loan to fall in arrears on loan payments. On conventional loans, they usually record a notice of default if the borrower falls 60 to 90 days overdue. On VA and FHA loans, they're usually more patient with the borrower and often wait up to six months before recording a notice of default.

In addition, conventional lenders normally charge higher late charges on a delinquent loan than lenders who fund VA and FHA loans. These late charges can run as high as 10 percent of each monthly payment.

The law provides the borrower a period for reinstatement of the loan, which means that within a certain period the loan can be brought up to date. This occurs when all monies in arrears, including all penalties, are paid in full. This period of reinstatement varies from state to state.

When a homeowner allows his home loan to go into arrears to the extent that the lender records a notice of default and foreclosure proceedings begin, he is now required to pay a sizable sum to make the loan current. Because the amount is substantial, the troubled homeowner will likely have to sell or allow the lender to foreclose.

Therefore, when you invest in a distressed property that has a VA or FHA loan attached, you'll benefit from the following:

- You can assume the existing loan without credit qualification.
- You can assume the existing loan for a small incidental fee.
- You won't be charged a prepayment penalty when you sell.
- The interest rate remains unchanged throughout the term of the loan.
- You can allow the next buyer to assume all the same benefits, or you can wrap the existing loan at a higher rate of interest.

If you invest in a distressed property that has a conventional loan with a due-on-sale clause, you'll have to:

- Be prepared to qualify for the loan.
- Pay a higher rate of interest if the existing rate is below the current market rate.

- Pay a prepayment penalty fee when you sell.
- Be prepared to pay off the existing loan, or get a new loan if the lender decides to exercise the due-on-sale clause.

Gather all the Data

What do you do after having located a property that appears profitable, made an appraisal, evaluated all the costs to renovate, and arrived at a price range you're prepared to offer? The next step is to answer the following questions:

- What are the names of the mortgagor and mortgagee or the trustor, trustee, and beneficiary?
- Is the loan in foreclosure a first or a second loan?
- When was it recorded, and for how much?
- If the loan in foreclosure is a second, who holds the first?
- Is the loan a conventional loan or a government-backed loan that can easily be assumed?
- How much is each loan in arrears?
- Are the taxes delinquent, and if so, how much?
- Are there other liens against the property?

You can find answers to most of these questions in the office of the county recorder where the subject property is located. All documentation involving real property is kept open to the public in the county recorder's office.

The recording process dates back to before the American Civil War. Now, as it did then, it provides the public a notice of important documentation in regard to real property. When it's time to verify pertinent data on a property in foreclosure, note that a first mortgage recorded has priority over liens recorded subsequently. In other words, except for tax liens, the first in line is first in right to any claims on the property.

The actual recording is done by the county recorder. When a deed is recorded, the county recorder will file a copy of that deed in the official records.

Closing the Deal

Before the troubled owner is prepared to make a deal, you must set the stage. The owner has to be convinced that you are a knowledgeable specialist in the field of real estate. You accomplish this during the initial stage of negotiations by demonstrating knowledge about the foreclosure process and by showing to the owner exactly what will happen if the condition is not remedied. The owner is also informed that it's too late to list the property for sale, and possibly too late to borrow additional funds. You can add that, by selling to you now, he can remedy the pending crisis, salvage his credit rating, and leave the burdensome property behind while departing with some cash in hand. Otherwise, the lender will acquire the property and everything will be lost, including his credit rating and accumulated equity.

The troubled owner should appreciate the investor's interest and feel relieved that help is near at hand. Troubled homeowners should feel they can speak openly when their financial difficulties are now out in the open. For that reason, the owner no longer feels someone is intruding, and he has no need to disguise the facts of his troubled financial condition. The troubled owner is prepared to act. Time is running out, and he has been alerted to the consequences. The owner now knows that you can remedy the situation better and faster than anyone else, and the owner is prepared to make a deal.

Price Declines with Time. Time is money. In no other realm of business can this fact be stated more emphatically. During the typical 90-day span of a foreclosure proceeding in which a property can still be reinstated under a deed of trust, offers to the troubled owner will vary. Offers during the first 30 days would be considerably higher than those made during the final days of redemption.

By the time a property reaches the final days of the 90-day reinstatement period, additional unpaid monthly installments have accumulated, and late charges have increased. The owner must be alerted to these facts; the quicker he acts to resolve the problem, the more he will get out of it.

Verification of Names. It's imperative that the seller's name on the deed be correct—if his legal signature is Anthony Thomas Jones, it's necessary to put down the name exactly as it is shown, not Tony Jones, or A.T. Jones—and that all the information on the deed transferring the property exactly match that on the original deed the seller received from the lending institution.

Once the owner has signed over the grant deed, you should immediately have it recorded at the county recorder. Later you can submit a copy of the grant deed to the title company. Immediately recording the grant deed assures you that any liens recorded against your newly acquired property will be invalid, as long as they're recorded after your name, and not before.

Finally, have the seller sign the Equity-Purchase Agreement, which will give you, the buyer, control of the property. (See Equity-Purchase Agreement form which follows.) This will be accomplished after completing final negotiations and checking that the property is actually transferable. Then the grant deed can be executed, signed by the seller, and properly notarized. Again, be sure that the grant deed is filled out exactly as the previous grant deed was. Once the grant deed is properly executed and notarized, take it to the county recorder to be recorded.

In conclusion, investing in foreclosures during the first and second phases requires, as you can see, much tedious research and preparation in order to complete a successful transaction. A much less complicated source of foreclosure property is available through institutional lenders in the following section on REO.

EQUITY-PURCHASE AGREEMENT

(This agreement is to be filled out in triplicate, with one copy issued to the seller, to the buyer, and one to the buyer's file records.)

Date _____ Address of subject property _____
_____ Lot # _____ Block _____ Tract _____

Lender's name _____ Loan # _____
Seller's name _____ Address _____

Buyer's name _____ Address _____

Buyer agrees to purchase and seller agrees to sell the equity in the above-described real property for the sum of _____
net to the seller, receipt of which is hereby acknowledged by the seller.

Buyer agrees to take title to the above-described property subject only to existing liens and encumbrances not exceeding _____
_____.

It is also mutually agreed that: _____
_____.

Seller is to deliver possession of subject property on or before _____
_____, 19____. If the property is not transferred to the buyer by the above-agreed date, all payments and further expenses incurred from that date forward shall be deducted from the net amount due to the seller at closing.

Buyer will pay all escrow, title, loan transfer, and closing costs.

Monthly payments on the above loan including, principal, interest, taxes, and insurance are _____.

Impounds for taxes and insurance, if any, are to be assigned without charge to buyer. Any unforeseen shortage in the impound account will be deducted from the net amount due seller at closing.

Seller will immediately execute a grant deed in favor of buyer, which the buyer has the right to record.

Seller will not remove any fixtures from the real property and will leave premises reasonably clean and in good condition.

Seller will allow buyer access to property for any reason prior to date of possession of the buyer.

Buyer will pay the balance of all funds due seller at closing after checking title, liens, and that the property is vacated.

Additions to this agreement: _____

_____

Buyer _____ Seller _____

Buyer _____ Seller _____

INVESTING IN REAL ESTATE OWNED (REO) PROPERTY

REO is real property that has been foreclosed on and that failed to sell at public auction. The financial institution now owns the property. One aspect of REO which makes it a superior investment when compared with property in the other two phases of foreclosure is that all clouds on the title have been removed through the act of foreclosure. In the process of acquiring the property, the financial institution has literally eradicated all outstanding liens, except for back taxes which had to be paid. The lender now owns the property free and clear. If you acquire REO, it will be free of encumbrances, except for deferred maintenance. You can usually buy REO property with a small down payment. The purchase can often be financed at interest rates below conventional rates, especially since the lender is also the seller and eager to unload the property. Sometimes it's possible to defer the first principal and interest payment up to six months, which will allow you to renovate the property and generate some income before the first payment is due. Also, it's not uncommon for the REO buyer to acquire an additional loan to pay for the cost of such renovation. And the financial institution will usually assume most of the closing costs.

The important thing to remember is that everything is very negotiable. Nothing is carved in stone regarding standard procedure for the buying and selling of REO.

To succeed at investing in REO, you need a special technique for dealing with REO managers. This is not an easy task because there has been a great deal of public interest in foreclosure property in the past 10 years, and potential REO buyers are constantly inquiring.

Typically, an inquiry from an uninformed member of the public is in the form of phone calls to REO departments, asking if any foreclosure property is available. So many people phone in that REO departments now give a stock reply: "Sorry, nothing available."

REO will usually be sold through an established real estate broker and to known investors who are personal friends the lender has done business with before. Thus, if you want to invest in REO, approach the REO department in person and meet its manager. Establishing such a personal relationship is the only viable way to have access to these potential bargains.

7 HOW TO BUY HUD-OWNED HOMES

Homes owned by the Department of Housing and Urban Development (HUD) are a great source of investment for anyone. These homes have previously been foreclosed on, were financed under VA and FHA loan programs, and are now owned by HUD. The following information is written for both investors and real estate brokers who might be interested in either listing or purchasing HUD-owned homes.

TYPES OF PROPERTIES AVAILABLE FROM HUD

- Vacant lots
- Single-family detached residence
- Duplex or two units on one lot
- Triplex—three units
- Four-plex—a four-unit building
- P.U.D.—A Planned Unit Development
- Condominiums

SALES POLICY

HUD sales policy is to sell to anyone regardless of race, color, creed, or sex who can meet the down-payment, credit, and certain other requirements. Not only prospective owner-occupants may offer to buy but investors may as well.

HUD lists properties for sale on an "open basis" with licensed real estate brokers. Offers to purchase are submitted by brokers on behalf of prospective purchasers, and HUD pays the broker's commission at closing. Showing properties to potential buyers, preparing the HUD-9548 Standard Real Estate Contract and Addenda, and following up on all paperwork required for closing a transaction are the primary responsibilities of the selling broker. Buyers may not submit offers directly to HUD except in circumstances where they cannot obtain the services of a licensed broker.

Buy Property in "As-Is" Condition
All HUD properties are sold as-is, without warranties. There will be no further alterations or additions made by the seller, and any other statements or representations made as to the condition of the property will not be binding on the seller. It is the buyer's responsibility to make a determination as to the condition of the property.

Financing the Sale
HUD properties are listed for sale, either with or without HUD mortgage insurance. For those properties listed "with HUD insurance," the buyer may seek an FHA-insured loan from a private lender and use the mortgage proceeds to buy the home from HUD. For properties listed "without HUD insurance," the terms are all cash to HUD in 30 days, with no contingencies for financing.

Mailing List
Real estate brokers wishing to be placed on the mailing list for the Broker's Information Package to participate in the sales of HUD properties must certify on the Public Information Mailing List Request (HUD-9556) that they will comply with Federal Fair Housing Laws and Affirmative Marketing Regulations. A broker's executed Form HUD-9556 must be on file at the HUD office before any offer or contract will be accepted from that broker. The Form HUD-9556 shall be renewed annually upon HUD's request.

Access to Properties
A HUD master key and lock box key can be obtained from any of the Area Management Brokers.

BROKER LISTING AND ADVERTISING PROCEDURES

Listings
Local HUD offices mail out weekly new listings of HUD properties directly to brokers on the HUD mailing list. Listings will include list

price, property description, bid opening date, and deadline date. With the possibility of errors in advertising, HUD reserves the right to reject any offer or bid.

Listing Price

The listing price of each property is HUD's estimate of fair market value. HUD will accept offers less than the listing price; however, it will only accept these offers providing the greatest net return. Listing price will include normal closing costs but not prorated taxes, prepaid interest, and the one-time prepaid mortgage insurance premium.

Broker Advertising

Broker advertising is encouraged by HUD as long as it's done according to the following guidelines:

- Price listed with broker cannot be any price other than the HUD-listed price.
- Broker cannot list until the property is officially listed by HUD.
- Context of broker advertising cannot be worded in such a way as to indicate that it is a distress sale.
- Brokers cannot word advertising to indicate that they are the sole source of HUD property data or that they have a favored listing advantage.
- Advertising must include the statement, "Properties are offered for sale to qualified buyers without regard to the buyer's race, color, religion, sex, or national origin."
- All advertising has to comply with the Truth-in-Lending Act.
- The words HUD or FHA cannot appear in the advertisement.
- No advertising is allowed that makes specific reference to down payment, loan term, or finance charges. Statements such as "no down" or "500 down," and "no closing costs" are not allowed by HUD. Furthermore, advertisements shall not set forth the interest rate nor specify the maximum mortgage available, either in amount or term. However, it is permissible to set forth general phrases such as "easy terms available" or "low down payment."

"For Sale" Signs

No signs or business cards are allowed to be placed in or on the property unless authorized by HUD. Only HUD's "For Sale" sign can be posted on the property. A "Sold" sign may be installed by the selling broker only after the broker is notified of the acceptance of the sales contract.

Open House

Brokers can hold an open house provided HUD receives and approves a letter of request from the broker. The open house is limited to two consecutive days, and property must be on the market at least 15 days before such an open house can be held.

AVAILABLE SALES PROGRAMS

HUD sells properties under two different programs, each of which has different terms and conditions. The following are features of each program.

As-Is Sales—All Cash Transactions

This program offers properties for sale in an unrepaired, or "as-is," condition for cash. Under this program the sale will not be contingent upon the buyer's ability to obtain financing.

Property Condition. The property is unrepaired and currently does not meet HUD's minimum standards for mortgage insurance. In addition, it may have local code violations. HUD does not allow repairs or modifications, even at the buyer's expense, on properties listed as-is before closing.

Warranty. Buyers should be cautioned that HUD provides no warranty, and that the property may have code violations.

Financing. HUD will provide financing costs for uninsured sales under the best offer addendum.

Earnest Money Deposit. Real estate brokers will collect the earnest money deposit, regardless of the method of sale. The following are the requirements: A minimum of $500, or 5 percent of the listing price, not to exceed $2,000. Sales of vacant lots require 50 percent of the listing price as the earnest money deposit.

Delivery of the deposit, along with sales contract and addenda are the responsibility of the selling broker.

Down Payment. Because the sale is all cash to HUD there is no down-payment requirement. However, if conventional financing is arranged, then the lender's requirements apply.

Tie Bids. A public drawing will resolve bids determined to be equally advantageous to HUD.

Time Allowed for Closing the Sale. Buyer is allowed 30 days to close the sale after HUD's signing of the sales contract.

Closing Costs. As described below in "Procedures for Bidding," HUD will pay or credit certain closing costs.

Insured Sales—Insured Financing Available

This program offers properties which are eligible for FHA-insured mortgage financing. Such financing requires the buyer to have acceptable mortgage credit, and the sale is contingent on the buyer's being approved. FHA-insured financing is not required and buyers may obtain other financing. However, if the buyer uses another form of financing, then the purchase becomes an "as-is, all cash" transaction.

Property Condition. Properties which HUD selects for sale with FHA insured financing appear to meet the intent of HUD's minimum property standards for existing dwellings, based on available repair estimates. Regardless, HUD does not certify that the property is without defects, and buyers should be cautioned to make their own determination of the property's condition before submitting an offer.

Warranty. Buyers should be cautioned that HUD provides no warranty whatsoever pertaining to condition of the property.

Financing. FHA-insured financing is available upon buyer qualification. Available programs are discussed below in "Sales Closing."

Earnest Money Deposit. Real estate brokers are required to collect a minimum $500 deposit, or 5 percent of the listing price not to exceed $2,000. Sales of vacant lots require 50 percent of the listing price as a deposit.

Down Payment. Owner-occupant buyers are required a down payment of 3 percent of the listing price up to $90,000. Investors are required to finance only 85 percent of the sales price. Sample computations are provided below under "Calculating Down Payments."

Owner-Occupant Priority. In the event of a tie bid, HUD will give priority to an owner-occupant's bid over that of an investor.

Time Allowed for Closing the Sale. The buyer is responsible for making sure that credit information is received by HUD as soon as possible after acceptance of the offer. Generally, the sale should be closed within 45 days after HUD's acceptance of the offer.

Closing Costs. As described below under "Procedures for Bidding," HUD will pay or credit certain closing costs.

Mortgage Insurance Premium. The MIP is now collected in one lump sum at the time of closing, either in cash or the mortgagor may finance it.

CALCULATING DOWN PAYMENTS

The following are examples of how to calculate down payments under the various programs available:

Insured Sales to Owner-Occupants
Only on Sales up to $90,000

Owner-occupants can finance 97 percent of the list price up to $90,000, and 90 percent of the bid exceeding the listing price. See the following example:

EXAMPLE 1

List price	$90,000
Buyer's bid	90,000
The down payment is calculated as follows:	
3% of $90,000	$ 2,700
Total down payment	$ 2,700

EXAMPLE 2

List price	$85,000
Bid price	88,000
The down payment is calculated as follows:	
3% of $85,000	$ 2,550
10% of bid above list price	300
The total down payment is	$ 2,850

Insured Sales to Investors

Investors are required a 15 percent down payment and can finance the balance of the sales price, up to local maximums.

EXAMPLE

List price	$60,000
Bid price	62,000
The down payment is calculated as follows:	
15% of $62,000	$ 9,300
Total down payment	$ 9,300

PROCEDURES FOR BIDDING

HUD properties are offered for sale under one of the previously mentioned programs on a competitive-bid basis. Should the property fail to generate a bid, or if all the bids are rejected, then the listing period will be extended for three working days after the regular bid opening. Sealed bids will be accepted until 3:30 P.M. of the third day. Opening of the bids will occur on the fourth working day at 9:00 A.M. at the HUD office. Appropriately marked and sealed envelopes are used for offers submitted under this procedure. (Note that these forms vary in each region, so it would be wise to call your local HUD office for information on the correct forms.)

HUD accepts those bids that produce the greatest net return. Greatest net return is calculated by deducting from the bid price (1) the dollar amounts that the buyer requests and (2) the sales commission HUD agrees to pay.

For as-is sales without insured financing, the deduction figure shall contain the sales commission and financing costs that are paid by HUD. Closing agent fee, deed recording fees, and owner's title policy are not included in the deduction.

For as-is sales with insured financing available, the deduction figure shall contain the sum of the sales commission and an amount which the buyer will expect HUD to pay toward the closing costs. At buyer's request, HUD will pay for loan-origination fees, discount points, and a credit report. HUD will not pay costs which in HUD's judgment are not reasonable or customary.

Selling brokers are required to prepare HUD-9548 Sales Contract showing the sum of costs the buyer expects HUD to pay and deducting this total from bid price to determine net return to HUD.

Closing of the sale will be conducted by HUD's closing agents, one of whom will be assigned to each sale. HUD will pay the closing agent's fee. The cost of this fee is not to be included in the calculation of the best-offer deduction on the addendum to the sales contract.

HUD will pay for title policy and deed recording fees on all closings and are *not* to be included as a closing cost on the addendum to the sales contract.

HUD will not, in any case, pay for a lender title policy or mortgage recording fees, or pay any other fees not specified in the contract.

Bid Example

As an example, let's assume that a property is listed for $50,000 on an insured-sale basis. HUD receives two bids on this particular property. The following example illustrates how HUD determines which of the two offers it will accept:

Bid #1, a selling broker investing for himself:	
Bid price	$50,000
Deduction (credit report)	50
Net to HUD	$49,500
Bid #2, an owner-occupant buyer:	
Bid price	$52,000
Deduction (commission, loan fees, and closing costs)	5,300
Net to HUD	$46,700

From the above illustration, the greatest net return to HUD came from bid #1, although bid #2 offered more for the property. Bidder #2 requested that HUD pay the 6 percent sales commission of $3,120 and $2,180 in loan fees and closing costs, for a total deduction of $5,300. Bidder #1 is requesting HUD to pay $50 for a credit report; however he does not request HUD to pay for financing costs. Also, Bidder #1 is a real estate broker, and in this case he elects to waive his commission, thus improving the competitiveness of his bid.

Bid Period

Generally, most HUD offices will accept sealed bids from prospective buyers beginning the day after the property is listed. The bid cut-off date is indicated on the listing, however, HUD reserves the right to change the bid period.

Sealed-bid Envelope

A sample bid envelope is shown on the following page. *Each individual envelope is to contain only one bid.* Bids are required to be in sealed envelopes, with the following information on the outside:

SAMPLE OF SEALED-BID ENVELOPE

Ace Realty Company
3985 Elm Street
Las Vegas, NV 89107

Dept. of Housing & Urban Development
Address of your local HUD office
where bids are accepted goes here.

Bid opening date: June 1, 1987
FHA # 367–754948–201
457 Main St   SEALED BID
Las Vegas, NV 89118
Mike Smith (Buyer) owner-occupant   DO NOT OPEN

- Name and address of selling broker.
- "SEALED BID—DO NOT OPEN." This statement is to be prominently displayed in the lower right-hand corner.
- Address of the property and FHA case number on the lower left-hand corner of the envelope.
- Date of bid opening.
- Name of buyer and whether he is an "investor" or "owner-occupant." If the buyer is not distinguished between the two, the bid will be treated as though from an investor.
- If the bid pertains to an "extended listing period," prominently note this expression on the envelope.

The Bid

The formal bid is to be completed on Form HUD-9548 Sales Contract. Attached to it is the addendum completed by the selling broker. The addendum contains the following information: property address, amount of the bid, requested total amount of selling costs to be paid by HUD, and the net to HUD after the deduction of these selling costs. Also indicate on the bid whether the buyer is an investor or owner-occupant.

To establish the highest bid received, those containing other than whole dollar amounts will be reduced to the nearest whole dollar amount. *Do not submit earnest money deposit with the bid.*

Bid Deadline
Bids must be in that particular HUD office usually by 3:30 P.M. on the advertised cut-off date unless otherwise indicated in the listing. *Bids must be hand delivered.*

Opening of Bids
The day after the deadline for submitting bids is usually the day most HUD offices conduct the bid opening. The opening of bids is a public event, and the time and place is announced in the weekly listings.

Winning Bid
The winning bid is that which provides the greatest net return to HUD, after considering the bid price and cost to HUD. Bids may be accepted which are less than stated list price. The winning bid is announced at the bid opening, and the representing broker is immediately notified. He will then be required to submit, within one working day, all sales documents and earnest money to the respective escrow closing agent. No applications will be returned.

Should the required documents from the winning broker fail to reach the escrow closing agent within the specified time, the bid will automatically be rejected. In the event only one offer is received by HUD and the representing broker fails to comply, the property will be relisted.

Submission of Sales Package
Include the following forms:

- Standard Retail Sales Contract HUD-9548, complete 5 parts
- Original and 4 copies of Addendum 21 Net Sheet
- Original and 4 copies of Addendum 18 Earnest Money Certification

HUD requires that all submitted forms be typed or printed legibly. Furthermore, the earnest money collected by the representing broker must be in the form of a cashier's check or money order made out to the broker.

Bids submitted under the "extended listing period" shall remain available for sale for three working days from the date of regular bid opening. Bids submitted under this procedure are to be marked "Extended Listing Period" and are to include the appropriate forms listed above.

The highest net bid, provided it is acceptable to HUD, shall be formally accepted on this same date. If identical net bids are received, a drawing of lots will be conducted on all cash sales. And the owner-occupant offer will receive priority over the investor offer.

ACCEPTANCE AND APPROVAL OF SALES CONTRACTS

Acceptance of all offers will be announced by a HUD official at the time of bid opening. At that time copies of the Sales Contract, Net Sheet, and Earnest Money Certification will be handed over to the broker representing the winning bid. The broker must then submit these copies along with the Earnest Money Deposit to the respective title company within one working day. Failure to comply within the allotted time will cause the offer to be voided and the Earnest Money Deposit to be forfeited while the property is relisted.

On acceptance of an as-is, all cash transaction, the buyer is required to close the sale within 30 days. If the closing does not occur within this time, the Earnest Money Deposit will be forfeited to HUD.

On acceptance of an as-is with insured financing transaction, it is important that the buyer and lender immediately get copies of the Sales Contract so as to secure financing. The buyer has the responsibility to get financing from a HUD-approved lender and is required to close the sale within 45 days. It is the lender's responsibility to submit a complete credit package to HUD as soon as possible. If the closing does not occur within 45 days, the Earnest Money Deposit will be forfeited to HUD.

Payment of Broker
Broker's commission will be paid from the sale proceeds at the time of closing. Sales commission to the broker is 6 percent of sales price (maximum).

Extension of Closing
In the event of unforeseen circumstances preventing the escrow from closing within the prescribed time frame, the broker, on behalf of the buyer, may ask HUD to extend the closing date of escrow. (The appro-

priate form is "Request For Extension of Closing Date and Fee Certification.") This request also incorporates the fee certification, currently at $13.50 per day, which can be granted for 15 days maximum. Before these requests for extensions can be implemented, they must be approved by a HUD official.

Cancellation of Transaction
Should a transaction be cancelled, the Notice of Cancellation will be forthcoming from the title company. This can only occur after HUD's review and determination to cancel.

Mortgage Credit Approval
A firm commitment will be sent by HUD to the title company and their Mortgage Credit Branch will send a firm commitment to the lender as well. No other notifications will be issued by HUD. It is the broker's responsibility when the closing instructions are received to notify the buyer that the loan application was approved, and that a closing date has been set.

Mortgage Credit Rejections
The lender will be notified by HUD by receipt of a copy of HUD-92026, Report on Application. The lender is then allowed up to three working days to submit any additional information regarding the acceptability of the prospective buyers. If, after considering this additional information, HUD still rejects the buyer's credit application, the sales contract will then be cancelled. The lender will be notified of any credit rejections.

Multiple Offers
Brokers are allowed to submit offers from different buyers on the same property.

Owner-occupant buyers. Brokers may submit bids by the same owner-occupant buyer on several properties subject to the same bid period. If all the offers submitted by a single buyer are on properties that others have also bid on, the first bid from that buyer accepted as highest eliminates the rest of his bids from consideration.

Investors. Brokers may also submit offers by the same investor on numerous properties subject to the same bid period. Should one of the offers submitted by the investor submitting several offers be the only one received on a particular property, its acceptance does not automatically eliminate from consideration the other offers.

Bidding Integrity

Prospective buyers and brokers shall not engage in practices designated to reduce the dollar return to HUD. In the event such practices are discovered, they will be referred to the Office of Inspector General for investigation. An example of such practice is the submission by one person of several offers under different names (usually names of other family members) to purchase the same property at different bid amounts.

SALES CLOSING

Broker's Role

It is the broker's role throughout the preclosing process to assist in overcoming difficulties encountered between HUD and the buyer, with the intention of expediting the sale by date of closing. Submission of information from the buyer should be prompt so as to avoid unnecessary delays. Contact with the HUD sales staff to resolve any problems should be made by the broker, not the buyer. All telephone calls to HUD from the buyer will be referred to the broker.

Buyer

Other than the down payment, the buyer is required to pay at closing: prorated taxes, mortgage insurance premium, prepaid interest, homeowner fees, and any other costs above those which HUD has agreed to pay. It is imperative that the broker fully apprise the buyer of all financial requirements regarding home ownership at the time of initial application.

Earnest Money Deposit Forfeiture

On properties eligible for insured mortgage financing, deposit forfeiture will not occur when either HUD or the lender fails to approve the buyer's credit. After credit has been approved on these properties, forfeiture will occur if the sale is not closed within 45 days.

On properties sold as-is, all cash transaction, deposit forfeiture will occur if closing does not take place within 30 days from HUD acceptance of the buyer's executed sales contract. Requests for refund of the earnest money deposit must be transmitted by the buyer through the broker who originally submitted the offer. All earnest money deposits are applied to the purchase price at closing.

Extensions
HUD will consider a request for extension of closing date which does not exceed 15 days. An extension fee of $13.50 per day is charged and payable at time of request. This amount is made payable to the respective title company and must be certified funds.

Obtaining Financing
It is solely the buyer's responsibility to obtain financing for all sales.

Time to Close
Sales closing of an as-is, all cash transaction, must be accomplished within 30 calendar days of HUD's acceptance of the sales contract.

Sales closing of an as-is, with insured financing transaction, must be accomplished within 45 days of HUD's acceptance of the sales contract.

Closing Agent
HUD will assign a closing agent to conduct each sale. The assigned closing agent will notify the broker and inform him of the location, date, and time of closing.

FHA MORTGAGE INSURANCE PROGRAMS AVAILABLE

The FHA has several programs available to finance property listed under the Insured Sale Program. A buyer can obtain an FHA loan from an institutional lender and use the loan proceeds to buy property from HUD. FHA-insured financing is available under any of the following three programs:

Section 203(b) Mortgage
This is the most common and popular 30-year, fixed-rate mortgage. Prior to January 1, 1987, all FHA loans were fully assumable. Under current law, FHA loans originated after this date can only be assumed after two years has elapsed from loan origination date.

Section 245: Graduated Payment Mortgage (GPM)
This loan program offers the borrower lower monthly payments initially, but they gradually increase over the term of the loan. Down-payment requirements are higher than Section 203(b) requirements; however this program allows the borrower to qualify at lower income levels. This program takes into consideration the borrower's future

income growth potential and the ability or inability to handle higher loan payments in the future.

Note that under a GPM "negative amortization" occurs, which means that during the early life of the loan, the borrower will actually owe more than originally borrowed. (This is the opposite effect of a standard "amortizing" loan, which reduces the principal amount owing as each payment is made.)

There are five payment plans available under the Graduated Payment Mortgage program. They are:

Plan I   Monthly mortgage payments increase 2.5 percent each year for five years.

Plan II   Monthly mortgage payments increase 5 percent each year for five years.

Plan III Monthly mortgage payments increase 7.5 percent each year for five years. (This plan is the most popular because it has the lowest initial monthly payment.)

Plan IV Monthly mortgage payments increase 2 percent each year for 10 years.

Plan V   Monthly mortgage payments increase 3 percent each year for 10 years.

Section 245(a): Growing Equity Mortgage (GEM)

Under this loan program, scheduled increases in monthly payments during the early years are applied directly to principal reduction. Therefore, unlike the GPM, there is no interest deferral or negative amortization associated with a GEM. As a result, GEMs have a much shorter term than the GPM or level-payment mortgages. This result of a shorter term substantially reduces the total cost of the loan to the borrower.

The down-payment requirements for the GEM are the same as Section 203(b) requirements. Payment Plans IV and V of the GPM are the only two plans used for the GEM.

For additional details on how to submit offers under these different financing programs, contact a mortgage company or institutional lender of your choice.

OTHER PROCEDURES AND POLICIES

Keys to Acquired Properties

HUD properties are equipped with keyed-alike locks, and only one master key is issued to each firm registered with HUD. Brokers who are issued a master key from HUD are required to make duplicate copies for their sales staff. Brokers are not to release master keys to prospective buyers, and buyers must be accompanied by a salesperson when entering HUD-owned properties.

No Pre-showing Before Listing
Showing of HUD properties prior to listing is prohibited.

No Occupancy Before Closing
Buyers are prohibited from occupying or working on HUD property before the sale is closed.

False Certification of Intent To Occupy
Buyers, other than investors, must certify their intent to occupy the purchased property. If FHA mortgagee insurance is sought, buyers other than investors are also required to certify their intent to occupy on the Mortgagee's Application and Firm Commitment (HUD-2900). False certifications from buyers are in violation of the law and may result in criminal prosecution.

HUD May Reject an Offer
HUD reserves the right to reject any bid, offer, or contract which is incorrectly drawn or which is submitted as a result of an incorrect listing or other error.

Contract Revision
Should a broker wish to revise a contract already submitted, he must submit a letter of request to HUD. This letter must be signed by the buyer, furnishing reasons for the revisions together with a revised contract complete with attachments and addenda. After review by HUD, the broker will then be advised on whether such revisions will be allowed.

Cancellation of Contracts
Buyers may request cancellation of their offer by submitting a written request, which includes reasons for cancellation, through the selling broker. The request will then be forwarded to HUD by the selling broker along with any other pertinent information not disclosed by the buyer. HUD will then make a determination regarding disposition of the earnest money deposit.

In the event a buyer requests cancellation of "All Cash, As-Is" contract at any time, or cancellation of an insured sale after acceptance by HUD, the earnest money deposit will be forfeited to HUD.

Exceptions will be made only in extreme cases and require full documentation and submission to HUD for final decision.

Procedures After Closing

All boarded-up material (all wood and hardware) becomes the property of the buyer after closing. It is not HUD's responsibility to remove boarded-up material, regardless of the type of sale. The padlock or lockbox is to be returned to the HUD Area Management Broker by the selling broker if they're to receive their commission check.

8 PROFITABLE INVESTMENT TECHNIQUES (What To Do with It Once You've Got It)

Numerous opportunities are available to you and a variety of methods can be used to accomplish certain investment goals. A few of the techniques which will be discussed are renting, lease-option, conversions, and selling the property outright. Once you've digested the available information, you can then direct your energy to the investment technique that will best suit your needs, ability, and long-term goals.

Keep in mind that real estate is essentially a long-term investment. Granted, big profits can be realized in short-term speculation; however to get the most from your investment you must look at your real estate holdings as a long-term investment. As long as you're patient and properly use the guidelines presented in this text, your chances of success at real estate investment are extremely high.

RENTING

After purchasing a property and renovating it into habitable condition, you have the option of either renting it out or selling it outright. If you decide to rent it, you have to decide whether to rent the property on a long-term lease or on a month-to-month rental agreement. First consider the pros and cons of each. The long-term lease (one year or more) has one primary advantage, that of securing the tenant over a long term and essentially limiting turnover and somewhat guaranteeing a stable flow of income over the term of the lease. (I say "somewhat guaranteeing" because in reality you cannot entirely guarantee that a long-term lease tenant won't move out without regard to lease obligations before his lease's expiration.)

There are two primary disadvantages to a long-term lease. The first is that you've restricted the saleability of the property because the lease would take priority over occupation rights should the property be sold before the lease expires. (The lease and all rights belonging to it are conveyed if the property is sold.) The second disadvantage is that under a long-term lease agreement you're restricted to the amount of rent you can charge by the terms of the lease.

Under a month-to-month rental agreement, about the only disadvantage is that your tenant is obligated only to occupy and pay rent in monthly increments. The advantages are that under such a short-term rental agreement you do not limit the saleability of the property, and you're entitled to increase the amount of rent after 30 days.

Simply renting out your property is definitely a proven method of realizing a reasonable yield on your investment. However, there is another method that offers tremendous returns and less hassles than simply renting out your property, and that method is lease option.

LEASE-OPTION: THE REAL MONEY MAKER

A lease with an option to purchase (lease-option) is a lease or a month-to-month rental agreement in which the tenant has a leasehold interest in the property with an option to purchase it. The option to purchase is a separate part of the agreement which specifies the price and terms of the contract. Under a typical lease-option agreement the owner (optionor) of a home would give the tenant (optionee) the option to purchase the rented home at a specified price, within a set period of time, and for an option fee (consideration).

Lease-option is not an entirely new concept. In fact owners of real property have been optioning their property for ages, but the use of options on residential property is relatively new. The use of an option, by itself without a lease, is very useful among raw land speculators. For example, a knowledgeable land speculator with inside information on future land use could tie up a large land parcel with an option to buy, then sell the option at a later date to a developer. Let's say that our knowledgeable speculator has inside information on the construction of a major thoroughfare or freeway. He could obtain an option, instead of purchasing a large parcel of undeveloped land from an uninformed owner at a bargain price, then later sell the option for a substantial profit to a developer once the construction of the highway commences.

I stumbled upon the lease-option concept out of pure necessity. (As has been said, "necessity is the mother of invention.") Anyway, as I mentioned before, I had a property in downtown Las Vegas which was experiencing more tenant-turnover than I could reasonably tolerate. So I experimented with the property during a vacancy and proceeded to run an ad in the paper offering "rent with option to buy."

The results from the rent-with-option-to-buy advertisement were overwhelming. I must have received ten times the calls I normally would have taken in under a "rental-only" situation. Within a week I had a qualified lease-option tenant residing in the property at a monthly rate $140 higher than the rental rate.

As time passed, I discovered all the other wonderful benefits the lease-option method had over renting. Besides the additional income, I noted that my lease-option tenants took better care of the occupied property than the renters. Further, should the holder of the option fail to exercise the option within the term of the agreement, he forfeits all option fees already paid. Furthermore, the benefits of those great low-interest rate assumable loans now came into play, since because it is built-in financing I could wrap all the existing loans with a higher overriding interest rate and make a profit on the differential. (See wrap-around mortgage.)

LEASE-OPTION

The following is an illustrated example of a property purchased several years ago in Las Vegas:

Purchase price:	$96,000
Down payment	10,000
Cost to renovate	1,200
Total investment	$11,200

Lease-option tenant paid $1,075 per month, which included option fee. Of the $1,075, rent was $850 and $225 was the option fee. Expenses on the property were as follows:

First loan (assumable) payable at $400 per month at 9%	$400
Second loan (assumable) payable at $485 per month at 9%	485
Taxes at $60 per month	60
Insurance at $30 per month	30
Total expenses	$975

Income on the preceding example is as follows: rent at $850, option fee of $225 for a total of $1,075. See the following:

Gross rent and option fee	$1,075
Less total expenses	975
Monthly cash flow	100
Plus equity build-up at $230 per month	230
Net monthly income	330
Net annual income ($330 × 12)	$3,960

Now we can calculate return on investment (yield). Return on investment is the total investment (down payment plus fix-up cost) divided into net annual income. Therefore:

$$\frac{\text{Net annual income of \$3,960}}{\text{Total investment of \$11,200}} = \text{Return on investment}$$

Return on investment = 35.36%

Return on investment is 35.36 percent, based on the period of time before the tenant exercises the option to purchase. Now observe the terms of the option agreement. Remember the purchase price was $96,000, however the tenant has the option to purchase at a specified price and term. The following is the illustrated option-purchase agreement.

Option-purchase price		$115,000
Less: one year of option fees ($225 × 12) = $2,700	$2,700	
Less: $2,300 cash to exercise the option	2,300	
Total down payment	5,000	5,000
Balance to be financed by 11.5% wrap-around mortgage		$110,000

Under terms of the option, the contract price is $115,000 less down payment (option fees + cash) of $5,000, and the balance to be paid over 20 years at 11.5 percent on a wrap-around mortgage. See the following example:

Balance owing to be
 financed at 11.5% on
 a wrap-around mortgage $110,000
Payment on wrap including

principal & interest	$1,173	
Taxes	60	
Insurance	30	
Total monthly payment	$1,263	

Once the tenant exercises the option, he will pay the seller $1,263 (less $90 taxes and insurance paid elsewhere) in monthly payment for 20 years. Now we can examine the results after the option is exercised.

Monthly payment including principal, interest, taxes and insurance		$1,263
Less taxes and insurance paid elsewhere		90
Total amount paid to seller		$1,173
The following items are what the seller continues to pay on: (seller pays)		
Existing first mortgage	$400	
Existing second mortgage	485	
Total seller payment	$885	885
Cash flow to seller		288
Plus equity build-up ($230 per month) as the existing loans pay down		230
Net income before taxes		$518

From the preceding example, the seller will net $518 per month on the initial $10,000 investment plus $1,200 in renovation costs for a total investment of $11,200. Now we can examine return on investment as follows:

Total investment	$11,200
Net income ($518 × 12 month)	6,216

To determine return on investment, you divide net income by the total investment which equals the yield or return on investment:

$6,216 ÷ $11,200 = 55.50% yield (Note that this yield will increase more because of the input of the $2300 down payment, which you will see in a later example).

The following is a simplified illustration of the mechanics of the lease-option:

LEASE-OPTION EXAMPLE
(Prior to exercising option)

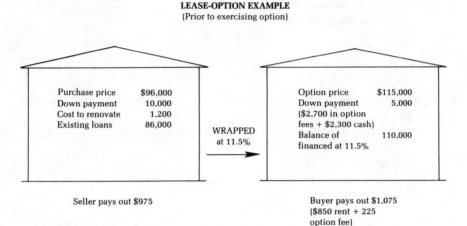

Purchase price	$96,000
Down payment	10,000
Cost to renovate	1,200
Existing loans	86,000

WRAPPED
at 11.5%

Option price	$115,000
Down payment	5,000
($2,700 in option	
fees + $2,300 cash)	
Balance of	110,000
financed at 11.5%	

Seller pays out $975

Buyer pays out $1,075
($850 rent + 225
option fee)

The following is what occurs when the lease-option tenant exercises the option to buy:

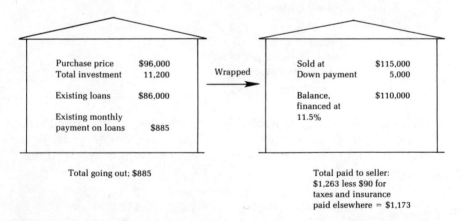

Purchase price	$96,000
Total investment	11,200
Existing loans	$86,000
Existing monthly	
payment on loans	$885

Wrapped

Sold at	$115,000
Down payment	5,000
Balance,	$110,000
financed at	
11.5%	

Total going out: $885

Total paid to seller:
$1,263 less $90 for
taxes and insurance
paid elsewhere = $1,173

From the above illustration, the seller continues to pay on existing loans only at $885 per month. Taxes and insurance of $90 are now paid by the buyer. The buyer pays the seller $1,173 per month on the new wrap-around mortgage at 11.5 percent for 20 years. The differential in monthly payments is $288 ($1,173 − $885), which represents the cash flow to the seller. When you add equity build-up of $230, the result is $518 in net income per month before income taxes.

Comparing return on investment, notice that the yield before the option is exercised is 35.36 percent as opposed to 55.50 percent after the option was exercised. Before I go any further, it is necessary to adjust the 55.50 percent notation, because in order to have the tenant exercise the option, an additional $2,300 cash payment was paid, which increases the net-income figure. Therefore, net income will be adjusted upwards to $8,516 ($6,216 + $2,300). Now we can calculate the actual return on investment, which will be substantially higher because of $2,300 added to net income after option is exercised. See the following example:

Total investment $11,200
Net income of $518 × 12 months + $2300 = $ 8,516
Return on investment = Net income divided by total
investment ($8,516 ÷ $11,200) = 76.04%

Now in the final comparison of return on investment, note that the final yield is more than twice that of the yield realized before the option was exercised (76.04 % compared with 35.36 %). This substantial differential is due to a number of factors. First, remember earlier in the text we discussed the importance of low-interest rate assumable loans? Well, here in the lease-option the value of these beneficial loans truly blossoms. A primary reason for their having such a profitable yield is that these low-interest loans are wrapped by a substantially higher loan. Second, the property is sold at a price $19,000 more than what was paid for it ($115,000 versus $96,000). And, third, when the option to purchase was exercised, the seller received $2,300 cash, which substantially added to the net income.

As you can see, the lease-option method can be a lucrative tool in real estate investment. Lease-option works. It has a broad market because many potential home buyers like the idea of making their down payment on the installment plan (paying option fees which apply toward the purchase of the home). You would be surprised at how many potential home buyers there are who earn enough income to afford to buy a home, however they don't have an adequate down payment to purchase it under other methods of financing.

The following is a sample Option-to-Purchase Agreement. Note that for the purpose of simplicity the option is kept separate from the lease for reasons to be discussed later. I also include the advertisement which ran in the *Las Vegas Review Journal* so that you can personally get a feel for the property in this example.

Rent with Option to Buy—Valley View & Warm Springs. Beautiful mini-ranch on half-acre zoned for horses with view of strip. 3 bedrooms & 2.5 baths beautifully decorated with oak floors & large country kitchen, den, fireplace & formal dining. Small orchard & covered patio, 2 car garage plus washer & dryer, frig & much more. $1,075. Call 555–1212.

SAMPLE OF OPTION TO PURCHASE

This option is made and entered into this 1st day of April, 1983, by and between Andy Seller, hereinafter called Landlord (owner), and Fred Buyer, hereinafter called Tenant.

Subject property is a single-family residence located at 3750 Arby, Las Vegas, Nevada 89107.

Landlord hereby agrees to grant an option to purchase to Tenant based on the following terms and conditions: Provided that Tenant shall not then be in default of leased property, Tenant to have option to purchase subject property at a price of $115,000 for one year beginning April 1, 1983, and expiring March 31, 1984.

Tenant agrees to pay a monthly option fee of $225 during the term of the option which will be applied toward the purchase price. Tenant further agrees to pay a down payment, including paid option fees, of $5,000 to exercise this option. Tenant agrees to finance the balance owing of $110,000 secured by a wrap-around mortgage in favor of Landowner at 11.5% per annum for 20 years at $1,173.08 per month.

Tenant agrees further to pay all taxes, insurance, and mortgage payments into a trust account for disbursement to all parties concerned and pay for such a trust account.

Tenant also agrees to purchase subject property in "as is" condition.

Landlord agrees to have all loans, taxes, and insurance current at time of execution of this agreement.

Both Landlord and Tenant agree to split all normal closing costs, except Tenant is to pay for title insurance.

Landlord further agrees to apply all security deposits and cleaning fees under the lease agreement toward down payment upon execution of this agreement.

The parties hereto have executed this option on this date first above written:

By _____ Landlord   By _____ Tenant

Important Note About Lease-Option

Under a lease-option agreement it is important that you maintain a month-to-month tenancy instead of a fixed rental agreement of one year or more. This is important because the tenant could decide not to exercise the option, and in so doing would cease making option payments. While at the same time the tenant has the right to occupy the premises under a long-term rental agreement, he is not obligated to pay the option fee. (Of course, if he does not pay the option fee, he no longer has the benefit of purchasing the house under the option agreement.) For example, assume that a tenant has a one-year lease with an option to purchase the property, in which case he pays rent plus an option fee. One month into the term of the lease he could decide not to exercise his option and cease making option payments; nevertheless he could continue making rental payments only while occupying the premises over the entire term of the lease. In doing so, he has substantially reduced the income flow from the property and you're stuck with him as a tenant only for the full term of the lease.

You can avoid this potential dilemma simply by maintaining month-to-month rental agreements which are related to an option to purchase. Then, if your tenant decides not to exercise the option, you won't be bound to the terms of a long-term lease agreement, and you could legally move him out in 30 days. Then replace him with someone with better intentions of eventually purchasing the property.

Put Everything in Writing

The exact terms of the option must be spelled out in the option. This way there will be no doubt or further negotiation. Both the buyer and seller will then know exactly whose responsibility it is to do what, and for how much.

An option to purchase can be as creative as the buyer and seller want it to be; however, it should be kept relatively simple to avoid any misunderstandings. Should by chance your tenant require a longer term on the option, you then essentially have two methods of determining the selling price for those periods. After the first year, you could set the option price at the existing price plus 1.5 times the consumer price index. The other alternative is to arbitrarily fix a selling price at which the tenant can buy the property during a specific term, such as $100,000 after one year, $110,000 after two years, and $120,000 after three years. (I, personally, prefer using the 1.5 times the CPI because historically real estate values tend to increase about 1.5 times the rate of inflation, which the CPI relates to.)

Advantages of Lease-Option

The lease-option concept is a very marketable technique, especially to potential home buyers who lack sufficient down-payment funds. Under lease-option the down payment can be paid on the installment plan through option fees. Your primary market then, is prospective home buyers who earn an adequate income to afford such housing, but lack a sufficient down payment to purchase a home under traditional financing methods.

Advantages to you, the seller, are tremendous when compared with renting or selling the property outright. First of all you save a sales commission—and on a $100,000 sale, that's $6,000 in savings. The second advantage is that while the tenant is in the option period, it is likely he will take better care of the property than he would under a rental-only condition. Furthermore, should the tenant not exercise the option, he would then forfeit all option fees already paid to you. In addition, certain tax advantages exist, that is, option fees are not taxable until the option is exercised, and selling on installment receives preferential tax treatment. Finally, under lease-option you profit from existing low-interest rate loans because when you sell, the existing loans are wrapped at a higher rate of interest, which generates a greater yield on investment.

Structuring the Option Agreement

The option agreement between you and your tenant can be as creative as the two parties involved want it to be; however, it should be precise, yet simple, to avoid misunderstandings between the parties. Be sure everything is in writing, leaving absolutely nothing to further negotiation.

Certain items, which in many cases might be considered unclear, such as the disposition of prepaid deposits and appliances (washer, dryer, and refrigerator), should be spelled out in the option agreement. For instance, both the cleaning and security deposit, which has been prepaid, can be applied toward the down payment as part of the agreement. And, the exact disposition of all appliances must be spelled out. In other words, if the appliances are to be included in the selling price, say so in the agreement; otherwise spell out the price you require for such items in the agreement.

Another consideration you have to make is what rate of interest to charge the buyer on the wrap-around mortgage? It makes good business sense to be fair and reasonable. Bear in mind that you will be competing with conventional lenders, because you are, in effect, acting as a conventional lender when you wrap existing loans, which in reality is creating a new loan. Then, as a rule of thumb, charge a rate of interest comparable to what conventional lenders are charging. But, remember, you do not charge loan origination fees! This means substantial savings to the prospective buyer. This is an important selling feature that deserves further attention. Conventional lenders have a variety of incidental charges that are added to the cost of originating a new loan. Remember the credit report at $75, appraisal at $150, 1 to 2 percent of the loan proceeds in points, plus the inconvenience and time to complete the required paper work? Therefore, remind your potential buyers of the convenience and cost-savings benefits they receive under the lease-option technique.

Finally, as part of your "tools of the trade," it will be necessary for you to purchase a book that covers interest rates and associated monthly loan payments. It is essentially a book of tables to calculate monthly loan payments for specific term and interest rate. Contemporary Books of Chicago publishes "Payment Tables For Monthly Mortgage Loans," or similar books are available in most bookstores.

SIX-MONTH ROLLOVER
100 PERCENT FINANCED

This investment technique is ideal for the investor with access to $50,000 to $100,000 in ready-cash working capital. It involves paying cash for property, quickly renovating it, then reselling at a profit wherein you recoup the entire investment on the sale. The ready-cash working capital can either be generated from your own funds, a partnership, or from a private or institutional lender. The principle behind this technique is the fact that a cash purchase commands a bargain price, especially when the seller is motivated to sell.

For example, let's say you have located a particular property which, if purchased for $67,000 cash and renovated, could be sold within six months for $100,000. For the benefit of this example we will presume that you have a lender that will lend you $75,000 for six months. The following will illustrate how the numbers work.

From the preceding example, the finance cost is calculated as follows: Typically, a financial institution or private lender would fund such a loan, including renovation costs, at 14 percent interest plus 4 points. The loan proceeds consist of $72,000, of which $67,000 represents the purchase price while $5,000 is the cost of renovation. Therefore, interest on $72,000 for six months is $5,040, plus 4 points at a cost of $2,880, for a total cost of $7,920. Although this cost to finance at first glance may seem excessive, this investment technique supports such a high finance cost because of such a great net profit, especially considering this technique was used without any of your own funds.

If by chance you were fortunate enough to possess enough ready cash to use the Six-Month Rollover technique without borrowing the

Six-month Rollover
100 Percent Financed

Purchase price		$ 67,000
Less the following expenses to acquire & renovate:		
Closing costs	$ 500	
Cost to renovate	5,000	
Cost to finance	7,920	
Tax and insurance (6 months)	300	
Utilities (6 months)	200	
Total expenses	$13,920	
Total expenses and purchase price		80,920
Property is sold for $100,000		100,000
Less the following selling expenses:		
Sales commission (6%)	$ 6,000	
Closing costs	500	
Total expenses and		
Purchase price	$80,920	
Total overall expense	$87,420	87,420
Net profit before taxes		$ 12,580

required working capital, then obviously you'd be that much farther ahead because you save $7,920 in finance charges.

The sales commission is another variable cost which was included in the analysis. Due to the short period of time involved in this technique, I usually find it necessary to pay a commission to procure a quick sale. However, if you can make a sale without the services of an agent, you would earn yourself an additional $6,000.

Ingredients of the Short-Term Rollover

The key to this investment technique, assuming the working capital is to be borrowed, is to have a lender tentatively arranged for such a transaction. Then, once a property you wish to invest in is located, you would make an offer contingent upon acquiring sufficient financing. If your offer is accepted, it would then be analyzed by your lender. Should the lender agree, then you're in business; if not, your offer would then be nullified because of the financing contingency inserted into your offer to purchase.

To profit from this technique, certain rules must be applied and only certain properties qualify. You can use this rule of thumb when purchasing a property: If you buy it at no more than two-thirds of its selling price after it's fixed up, you made a good deal. For instance, in the preceding example the purchase price was $67,000 which is two-thirds the selling price of $100,000. If you purchased a home for $80,000, the selling price would have to be $120,000 to incorporate the two-thirds ratio.

Properties which best qualify are those that have a substantial amount of equity and the seller is unwilling to carry back a note; they require much renovation, yet are sound in structure and overall construction. A large amount of equity means that the seller, has in most cases, owned the property for an extended period. Since he bought the property for substantially less many years ago and is unwilling to carry a note or renovate the property, he would be inclined to sell at a bargain price in order to be totally cashed out of the property.

Let's detail this method again just to illustrate exactly what happens. To begin with, you need a lender who will advance the entire proceeds, including renovation capital. You purchase the property using the loan proceeds to pay all existing loans in full and to pay the seller cash for his equity. The lender will then create a new first mortgage on the subject property. With the additional renovation capital, you refurbish the property, then sell at a substantial profit. When the property is sold, you pay off the lender with a new first mortgage, and you earn the differential, which is the profit.

In conclusion, when you purchase a property and intend to sell it within one year, you can earn substantial savings on title insurance. Most title companies will allow you to pay an additional retainer, usually $50, which will be the total cost of title insurance when you sell. The cost of such a policy without the retainer is approximately $500, so you can save $450 by paying in advance for the retainer when you purchase the property.

CONVERSIONS

Apartments now functioning as condominiums. . . . Gas stations now operating as retail outlets (Seven-Elevens). . . . Old homes converted to prime office space. . . . What was once prime farm acreage is now a sprawling urban shopping center. These phenomena are examples of changing usage of both land and buildings brought about by a city's outward growth.

An oversupply of gas stations throughout the city serves as another example. Because of overwhelming competition among these service stations, the more unprofitable ones shut down and remain vacant, while others are converted to needed parking lots and retail outlets.

Conversions provide boundless opportunities for the creative investor. Converting an old house located in the downtown area can be very profitable, because prime office space rents at twice the rental rate of residential housing, and in certain areas of the country it is even more.

Several years ago, when I worked for Wolverine Development in Lansing, Michigan, the company was involved with investing in strategic corner locations in the path of the city's outward growth. We would purchase single-family homes on a potentially good corner location, with the long-term intention of converting it to a more profitable rental use. This method had a great advantage over investing in similarly located vacant land because improved property can generate income and be depreciated.

As you can see, converting land use and its buildings is like turning straw into gold. But how can you take advantage of these changes in land use? Begin by obtaining an overall zoning map from your city's planning department. Each area within the city limit has a particular zoning (residential, multi-unit, agricultural, commercial, and industrial) limiting its land use. Ideally, a good conversion prospect would be a residential home already located within a commercial zone. Of course, if the property you wish to convert, that is, a residential home located in a residential zone, would require a change in zoning to accomplish your objective. Applying for a variance or zoning change requires a change in zoning law, which normally entails much time and effort. Properties which are the simplest to convert are those that are adjacent to the zoning which you wish to convert to. If you're interested in pursuing this matter any further, check with your local planning department and inquire into the necessary procedure.

Condominium Conversion

To convert an apartment building into individual condominium units, you would need, ideally, to purchase the apartments inexpensively enough so that each unit will easily convert to a saleable condo. Because of legal procedures and incidental costs to convert, not to mention the time and effort required, a two-to-one rule of thumb is required. This means that the sales price of the converted condo should be at least twice that of the per-unit purchase price of the apartment building. For example, if the purchase price of the apartment building is $40,000 per unit, then the sales price of each individual condo must be at least $80,000. This two-to-one markup is necessary so as to absorb the incidental costs incurred plus the time and effort necessary to make such a conversion.

You must also consider the legal procedures necessary to accomplish condominium conversion. First, the city has to approve the change in use. You will be required to submit plans explaining exactly how you intend to make the conversion. Should the city consider your plans adequate, it will approve the conversion. If not, certain changes, such as additional parking or bathrooms, would be needed before you get permission from the city.

Before going ahead with plans for a condo conversion, analyze the local area to determine what comparable condos are selling for. If you can purchase an apartment building at a low enough price, then renovate and sell the converted units and earn a profit while absorbing time and costs to convert, then by all means go ahead with your plans.

Converting Apartments to Office Space

Office space rents for twice the rental rate of comparable apartment rental space. Just from this observation it would appear highly profitable to convert apartments to office space. But before you go ahead with such a conversion, you should consider some important questions:

- Is the property you wish to convert within a commercial zone? If not, can it easily be changed to the proper zoning?
- What is the current vacancy rate for office space in the area of the subject property? If too much space is already available, it would be unwise to convert.
- Do you have adequate parking for office space? Typically, the city will require one parking space for every 500 square feet of rentable office space.
- How much will it cost to convert? Could you borrow the money to finance such a conversion? And, finally, will the cost, legal procedures, and time and effort be worth the eventual profit you will realize?

Study the situation carefully. Thoroughly analyze the finances of the projected conversion. Keep in tune with the requirements given, and if you can convert and finance at a reasonable cost and still earn a substantial profit, then go ahead with your plans.

SELLING THE INVESTMENT OUTRIGHT

Instead of renting or lease-optioning your property, you also have the alternative of selling it. Selling the property which you've invested time, money, and effort in has essentially one advantage, and several glaring disadvantages. The one advantage is you immediately realize the profit after the sale, which means you'll have plenty of ready cash available. But, this is only an advantage if you have a good place to reinvest the proceeds in.

Bear in mind that real estate is essentially a long-term investment. To get the most for your money, property has to be bought at the right price, then renovated, so a profit can be earned year after year.

Envision your real estate investments as tiny seedlings planted throughout a sprawling orchard which you nurture. While you feed and water the existing seedlings, you continue to plant new seedlings. In reality, your seedlings are individual properties invested in throughout the city (the orchard), and you nurture them through renovation (giving new life), and in turn these seedlings grow to be giant redwoods. And, while your seedlings are growing up to be giant redwoods, in return for all the loving care you've given them, they pay you back with generous amounts of appreciation, not to mention tax-free income.

Now consider the disadvantages of selling the property. The most undesirable aspect of such a sale is that now you have to find another investment for the proceeds from the sale. You could put the money in savings, but who wants to earn a meager 5 percent? Realistically, you have to seek out a new real estate money-maker which can earn more than a thin 5 percent.

The other glaring disadvantage of selling the property is that, under certain conditions, income taxes have to be paid on the gain from the sale. (Income taxes can be deferred if within a year of the sale another property of greater value is purchased.) Note that before the Tax Reform Act of 1986, capital gains rules allowed the taxpayer to defer 60 percent of the gain from a sale. However, under the new law, preferential treatment of capital gains has been repealed, which means the gain from the sale of real estate is now treated as ordinary income.

Let's face it, an outright sale eliminates property accumulation and makes ready cash available for frivolous spending. New cars, boats, and vacations are nice, but hardly a wise investment for someone who wants to be financially independent by the age of forty.

These are good reasons for not selling the property, and these reasons apply most of the time, but sometimes they do not, and those are the times when you should sell the property.

For example, you need the cash to better your investment position, so you decide to sell. The property you want is a real bargain: the price is right, the terms are great, but you don't have the down payment. For any number of reasons you're against taking out a loan or taking on a partner with cash. Under these circumstances you might consider selling one of your properties to raise the necessary down payment, especially if it improves your financial condition. Let's assume that you could sell one of your properties in which you have a large equity position. The property you want is a 20-unit apartment building, and the owner requires $30,000 down. You decide that by selling your property and buying the apartment building, you'll substantially increase your cash flow and leverage. You then have definitely improved your financial condition.

9 MAKING THE OFFER

On average, real estate traditionally sells for 5 percent below its asking price. This doesn't mean, however, that you should make all your offers at 5 percent below the list price. Five percent only represents an average, which means some properties sell for 10 percent below asking price, while others may sell exactly at list price. Incidentally, certain properties have been known to sell above the listed price, especially when more than one interested party gets involved and a frenzied "bidding war" begins.

Which brings us to an important point. Usually the only party that benefits when two or more people are competing to buy an individual property is the seller. Try to avoid getting involved when other buyers are making offers on the same property. The influx of the additional competition makes it too difficult to procure a good buy. Besides, why bother with competition when several other potential bargains are available from motivated sellers? You only need to locate them.

PREPARING TO NEGOTIATE

At this point you're bargain hunting, searching the local want ads and cruising the neighborhood looking for a good buy. And, finally, you find one that looks promising. It's for sale by the owner and has all the ingredients of a good buy (fixer-upper, assumable financing, low interest rate, and the seller appears motivated). Now what do you do? Negotiations begin right here, but wait . . . The most important time you'll ever experience investing in real estate is the next hour you spend negotiating with the seller. And, the first person to mention a number loses. If you're patient (probably the greatest virtue of a good negotiator) and wait long enough, the seller will mention a number, thus weakening his position. A motivated seller becomes even more anxious in the presence of a patient negotiator.

The scenario of initial negotiations between buyer and seller could begin like this: The seller might say, "How much would you give me for the property?" If the buyer replies with a price, he loses. Because, the price the buyer offers might be substantially above what the seller is willing to accept, and consequently the buyer has just overpaid for the property.

The information you require from the seller is the lowest price he would be willing to accept. But how do you find this out? or you could initiate negotiations by saying, "What is the least amount you will accept for the property?" When the seller replies with a price, you then have a figure which you can either accept or bargain further with.

Whatever you and the seller finally agree on, you are going to have to live with. So it is absolutely imperative that you be fully informed of comparable values and bargain for a good deal.

Before initial negotiations even begin, you must establish the maximum dollar amount you would pay for the property. This price represents your final offer. Anything above this price is not worth paying, because then the property is no longer a bargain. The price you actually pay should be substantially below the established maximum, for then you've definitely made a good investment.

NEGOTIATING

Ideally, negotiations are simplified when the seller is highly motivated, wanting to sell for any number of reasons. You already know the seller's asking price and terms. You know, from your homework, that similar homes in the area sell for between $62,000 and $84,000, and the seller is asking $80,000. Now you have a basis to work from.

If at this point the seller initiates negotiations with a statement like, "The least I would take is $75,000 with a $10,000 down payment," you reply with patient silence. Now at least you know the seller is flexible. You could accept this price and terms, but there is definitely more room for negotiation. The seller starts getting anxious and says, "Well, I guess I could take $72,000, but not a penny less." Notice that you haven't said a thing, and already the seller has come down in price from the original asking price of $80,000, to $75,000, and now to $72,000. Let the seller do the talking. The silence is working beautifully and weakening the seller's position.

Bargaining to reach agreement is what negotiating is all about. Unless you're prepared to pay all cash, and at the seller's asking price, you will be bargaining for price and terms. As a general rule, if a seller is firm on price, then negotiate terms. If he is firm on terms, then negotiate price. If the seller is firm on neither, then negotiate both. If he is firm on both, then start looking for another investment (unless of course the asking price is just too good to pass up, which is unlikely).

MAKING THE OFFER

Consider at this point what you can offer the seller in terms of a down payment. A total cash down payment is not always necessary to consummate a sale. Personal property items, such as vehicles, boats, recreational vehicles, furniture, and appliances can often be used instead of cash. During earlier negotiations with the seller, you might have noticed that he's going to retire shortly; he might therefore consider a boat or RV for his equity in the property. Or instead of looking for cash he might be looking for income, which means you could offer a secured mortgage for his equity in the property.

Once you have a good idea of what the seller wants out of his property, you start negotiating the price. Get the price as low as you possibly can before doing anything else. Next you negotiate the down payment, keeping it as small as possible, since you need to preserve your cash to buy and renovate additional properties. Your available cash is a valuable asset; it's working capital, and without it you're out of business. Remember the principle of leverage: the less you have invested in the property, the more leverage you will have, and the greater your return on investment will be.

Deposit Receipt and Offer To Purchase

Now that negotiations are complete and the price and terms are agreed upon, it's time to put your offer in writing. The written offer is to be completed on the Deposit Receipt and Offer to Purchase form which follows at the conclusion of this chapter. Pertinent information can be transcribed on to this form from the Purchase Agreement Checklist, which was previously completed in the "how to sell" chapter. The following are individual guidelines for each important paragraph within the Deposit Receipt and Offer to Purchase form.

Amount of Earnest-Money Deposit

Any amount ranging from $100 to $3,000 would be an appropriate amount for the earnest-money deposit. The recommended amount is $100 for a deposit, so as to limit your liability. Why? Because in the event you're forced, for whatever reason, to default on the transaction, you need to keep your losses to a minimum. Should your offer be accepted, it is likely that the seller, or the seller's agent, will require a larger deposit to secure the transaction and protect his interest.

Balance of Purchase Price

In this paragraph, certain contingencies and the total payment of the purchase price of the property less the earnest-money deposit are described. The following are sample clauses describing how the purchase price will be paid:

- Buyer to assume existing first deed of trust at 9 percent per annum at $487 per month, with an approximate balance owing of $40,000.
- The remaining balance of $42,000 to be carried by the seller in the form of a second deed of trust payable at 9 percent per annum, fully amortized over 15 years, payable at $438 or more per month.

The following clause is a "subject-to" clause, which is a contingency inserted into the offer to require certain limitations and conditions that must be fulfilled before the offer is valid. This particular clause is used when new financing is required.

- Subject to buyer's obtaining a new first mortgage in the amount of $_____ payable at approximately $_____ per month including interest at _____ percent per annum.

This subject-to clause limits your liability. If you do not obtain financing, you get your deposit back.

The following subject-to clause covers appliances and other working equipment.

- Subject-to all equipment, including appliances, pertaining to the operation of the building being in good working order as of the day of closing.

A subject-to clause can cover almost anything, and you need certain ones to limit your liability. However, keep in mind that the seller's agent will attempt to eliminate excessive contingencies, because they tend to complicate what would otherwise be a simple closing.

Closing Date

In the event you're assuming existing financing without qualification, closing can easily take place within 30 days. If new conventional financing is required, allow at least 45 days to close. Under FHA or VA financing, usually 60 days is required to close.

Should you purchase an occupied rental property, engineer the closing date to coincide with the date the rents are due. You are rarely obligated to pay mortgage payments until 30 days after closing, but you are entitled to collect all the rents and retain deposits on the first day of ownership.

COUNTEROFFERS

Commonly the seller will find your initial offer unacceptable and in most cases will propose a counteroffer. Once a counteroffer is proposed, the initial offer is terminated.

The procedure of offer/counteroffer is important because it brings out the flexibility of both buyer and seller. Always remember that you should have a maximum dollar amount you will pay. In the event you're confronted with an inflexible seller, don't waste any more of your time. Chalk up your effort and time to experience and find another property. If, on the other hand, the property remains an excellent buy, then continue to pursue an agreement. Quite often, especially when a good buy is at hand, a property is sold right out from under a negotiating buyer because he persisted in demanding excessive concessions from the seller.

Once the Deposit Receipt and Offer to Purchase is completed, it has to be placed in escrow in preparation for the final closing. If you sold the property without the services of a broker, you are then required to locate a reputable escrow agent and open escrow yourself.

In conclusion, practice the art of negotiating and making offers. Don't be disappointed if your initial offerings fail to purchase a bargain-priced property. You'll benefit from the experience which will enhance your future ability to make a great buy at a later time.

The following is a sample form of the Deposit Receipt and Offer to Purchase.

DEPOSIT RECEIPT AND OFFER TO PURCHASE

Date: _____, 19 ____

Received from _____

the sum of _____ dollars ($_____) in the form

of [ ] cash [ ] note [ ] check to be deposited and presented for payment upon acceptance of this offer, to secure and apply toward the purchase of the following described property: _____

_____

commonly known as _____

for the purchase price of _____ dollars ($_____)

subject to conditions, restrictions, reservations, and rights-of-way now on record, if any.

Balance of the purchase price is to be paid as follows:

_____

_____

_____

_____

_____

_____

It is hereby agreed:

1. That in the event the Buyer shall fail to complete the purchase as herein provided, the amount paid herewith may at the option of the Seller, be retained as the consideration for execution of this agreement.

2. That an escrow is to be opened with _____ or other designated escrow agent, who will be instructed to prorate current taxes, insurance, rents, sewer-use fees, and interest (if any) of subject property to _____ unless otherwise provided herein. The amount of bond assessments, if any, which is a lien or assessed against said property to become a lien, shall be [ ] paid by Seller, or [ ] assumed by the Buyer (check one).

3. That escrow is to close on or before _____, and possession of premises shall be given on _____.

4. That certain items of personal property, attached hereto as Exhibit "A," are included in the total purchase price as shown above and are to remain with the property.

5. That final vesting to be: _____

_____

and that evidence of this title to be in the form of owner's policy of title insurance furnished by _____ and paid for by the Seller. Escrow fees are customarily charged in the State of _____ and are to be divided equally between Buyer and Seller, unless otherwise stated. In the event of the cancellation and/or default of this contract, the defaulting party shall be liable for all fees or charges incurred when that party is otherwise obligated to perform under this contract.

6. That this payment of earnest money is made subject to the approval of the Seller and unless so approved and communicated to the Buyer by (date-time) _____ and subsequently delivered, the return of

the money, upon demand by the Buyer, shall cancel this agreement without damages to the undersigned. In the event of a dispute between the parties regarding the disposition of the monies paid pursuant to this contract, the broker of the designated escrow agent holding said monies shall retain possession of such funds without liability and shall not be obligated to dispose of those funds until there is an agreement between the parties, or by court order to do so.

7. That the terms written in this Offer and Receipt constitute the entire contract between the Buyer and Seller and that no oral statements made by the broker relative to this transaction shall be construed to be part of this transaction unless incorporated in writing herein.

8. That we will carry out and fulfill the terms and conditions as specified herein. If either party fails to do so, he or she agrees to pay the expenses of enforcing this agreement, including reasonable attorney fees.

9. That Buyer and Seller will give notice to the broker if any changes are made to this agreement.

By: _____ Agent/Broker

I agree to purchase the above-described property on the terms and conditions herein stated:

_____ (Buyer)
_____ (Buyer)

Seller

I agree to sell the above-described property on the terms and conditions herein stated, and agree to pay the above-signed broker as commission $ _____ _____, or one-half of the deposit should same be forfeited by purchaser, provided said amount shall not exceed the full amount of said commission.

_____ (Seller)
_____ (Seller)

Executed this _____, day of _____, 19 ____,
at _____ AM/PM

10 PROPERTY MANAGEMENT:
One Person's Dilemma is Another's Goldmine

Real estate is for sale, in many cases, because of improper management skills, which usually cause the novice landlord unwarranted headaches and needless frustration. Vacancies, late-paying tenants, vandalism, lack of money to pay the bills on time, all these items of nuisance cause many landlords to sell their properties when it really wasn't necessary. Whatever the case, these negative aspects present a great opportunity for the shrewd investor who has the skills to overcome such problems.

I acquired most of my own property management experience when I worked as a resident manager of a 363-apartment unit. My employer owned and operated 28 similar projects throughout the country, and each property was a syndicated partnership operating very profitably with less than 2 percent vacancy nationally. This company operated efficiently (the national vacancy rate is 5 %) because it stayed on top of things. Proper maintenance, rent collection, advertising, and so on—all these functions ran like a precision-made Swiss watch.

The company had its own property management book, in excess of 900 pages, which specifically directed the manager of each project on handling just about any situation that arose. From this experience I have written a chapter of guidelines to assist anyone in managing residential-income property. It is hardly as thorough as the 900-page text mentioned above; however I endeavored to present the highlights from what I absorbed. If you own or manage, or plan to own or manage, any form of residential real estate, you would be wise to learn these property management skills forthwith. By doing so, you can gain the ability to convert an abused, under-rented, half-vacant property into a well-run, money-making goldmine with a minimum of frustration.

PROPERTY MANAGEMENT COMPANIES

Professional real estate management companies have the responsibility to operate the building, pay all the expenses, keep it rented, maintain it, and send the owner a monthly report of their activities, along with a check for any proceeds. They charge anywhere from 5 to 10 percent of the gross collected rents for their services, depending on the size and character of the building being managed.

If you own one rental, or many individual, rentals, it would probably be smart to manage them yourself. However, if you plan to be an absentee landlord and reside far enough away from your rentals that it would not be practical to manage them yourself, then you should consider hiring a management company.

Like any other business, property management companies have their share of professionally run companies as well as incompetently run ones, but, for the most part, they earn their fees. However, the incompetent companies not only operate inefficiently, but in so doing they also cheat the owners of deserving profits. Just to mention a few larcenous schemes that crooked property managers can use to bilk unsuspecting property owners: invoicing the owner for repair expenses which in fact do not exist; renting out a vacant unit while collecting the rent and declaring to the owner that the unit is still vacant; and charging owners excessive amounts for painting and repairs and keeping the overcharge themselves.

Putting property management into the hands of a professional firm will cost you 10 percent of the gross collected rents and probably a lot more. No one can operate your properties as efficiently as you can, because you have an important investment to protect and nurture. Besides, why turn the responsibility of operating your properties over to someone else and take the risk of being ripped-off by less than competent managers? If you take the time to learn the skills required to efficiently manage your own properties—and these skills are all included in this text—it won't be necessary to hire a management company. In conclusion, about the only time I would consider hiring a management company would be in the event I was no longer physically capable to oversee my properties or when I had to relocate to another area and it was no longer practical to manage them myself.

FURNISHED VERSUS UNFURNISHED UNITS

Generally speaking, if you are renting single-family homes, it will be to your advantage to keep your units unfurnished. If you do supply furniture, of course you can charge more in rent for the use of the furniture; however it is then your responsibility to maintain and insure it from theft and fire damage. The major disadvantage of supplying furniture to your tenants is the fact that it creates more turnover. A rented home completely furnished is very easy to get up and move away from. On the other hand, a rented home where the tenant supplies his own furnishings requires much more of an effort to move into and out of. Invariably, once a tenant takes the time, effort, and expense to move all his belongings into a home, it is very likely he plans to stay awhile.

On the other hand, certain types of rental units require furniture in order to maintain a high-occupancy rate. If you happen to own single or studio-type apartments which tend to thrive on more transient clientele, then supplying adequate furnishings would be to your advantage.

APPLIANCES

Items such as refrigerators, washers, and dryers are expensive to purchase and maintain, but when they are offered as an amenity with your rental unit, they do offer saleability to your rental. It has been my experience that if you have the opportunity to buy these appliances at bargain prices as part of the purchase of the entire property you invest in, then by all means do so. The responsibility of maintenance and repair of such appliances can mostly be turned over to your tenants via the "no-hassle $100 deductible repair clause" inserted into your rental agreement. This particular clause states that "the first $100 in repair of the rented property, including appliances, is the tenant's responsibility." (More on the no-hassle clause later on in this chapter.)

If you own a multi-unit apartment building with nine or more rental units, you have to consider whether to supply a laundry facility with coin-operated washers and dryers, and whether you should buy or lease the equipment. In smaller buildings, eight rental units or less, supplying washers and dryers would not be economically practical because usage would not pay for the cost of the utilities to run the machines.

Should you buy the coin-operated equipment, they would probably pay for themselves within two years. That's the good part. However, you have to maintain the equipment and be responsible for acts of vandalism and the unauthorized removal of coins from your machines.

On the other hand, you could lease your laundry equipment from a reputable rental company. This way the leasing company would be responsible for supplying and maintaining the equipment while at the same time collecting coins from the machines. The owner would be responsible for paying the utilities. Generally, when you lease laundry equipment, the leasing company retains 60 percent of the gross receipts and remits the remaining 40 percent to the owner. Precautionary measures can be taken so that a responsible person oversees the removal of coins from the rented equipment in order to help eliminate the temptation of skimming from the coin boxes.

UTILITIES AND TRASH REMOVAL

For the tenant who rents single-family residences or condominiums, it is his responsibility to pay for the utilities and the trash removal. However, in most apartment buildings, especially the later models, there are separate meters for gas and electricity consumption, and the respective companies bill the individual tenants. But the owner of the building is responsible for paying the water bill. When separate meters are not available for gas and electricity, the owner must add the cost of these items to the rent. Furthermore, trash removal from multi-unit buildings is best paid for by the owner so as to maintain a cleaner building and avoid friction with the tenants as to whose responsibility it is.

MAINTENANCE AND REPAIR TIPS

As an owner of rental property, it is often wise to look like a handyman when you approach your property rather than a chauffeur-driven Rockefeller. The aim should be to appear like a hard-working person, not a high-rolling big shot. You'll find that being more discreet will get you your rents faster and will help to deter tenants' petty complaints.

You must keep vacancy rates at a minimum in order to maintain a maximum income level throughout the operation of all your properties. By adequately maintaining your units and keeping your present tenants satisfied within reason, you can reduce the desire on their part to move elsewhere. Of course you have no control over a situation when a good paying tenant is requested by his employer to relocate to another city. But you can retain good tenants by properly preserving your buildings. It begins by being reasonable about your tenants' complaints and requests.

It is the owner's responsibility to keep everything in working order (except if you have a "no-hassle" $100 deductible, tenant-pays clause in your lease), and at the same time the tenant should be responsible for not misusing the rental property. Painting, carpet shampooing, and plumbing stoppages are the owner's responsibility, but only when the tenant is giving reasonable care to the property. When a tenant continues to pour grease down the kitchen drain, or allows the kids to plug up the toilet with small toys, the tenant becomes responsible for the costs of repair instead of the owner.

Usually a year elapses before a tenant might begin making requests for any refurbishment of the unit, assuming the unit was in tip-top shape initially. A wall or two may require a new coat of paint, old carpeting may need replacing, or possibly only a carpet cleaning is requested. Whatever the case, it is at this point that you cannot ignore a tenant's request to have something done. If you do ignore him, you could lose a good paying tenant. If your tenant moves out because you wouldn't paint the kitchen, it will cost you much more than a meager paint job. Should he move to another unit, you not only have to prepare the unit for a new tenant, but you will probably experience an extended vacancy loss. Therefore, instead of spending a few dollars for a kitchen paint job, you could spend much more by re-renting the unit to a new tenant. Refurbishing the entire unit for a new tenant could cost $200 or more, plus the additional expense of lost revenue with a vacant unit.

It is essential to the profitability of your total operation—whether it is merely a single rental home or numerous apartment buildings— that you preserve and maintain your properties. By doing so you will not only keep quality tenants satisfied, but your occupancy rate and related profits will be kept at a maximum level as well. Then your properties will reflect their maximum value until they are eventually sold.

When I first started in the rental real estate business, the only experience I had in repairing things was high school Shop 101, which basically taught me how to tighten loose screws and sand wood. As a novice investor, I hired most of the required repair work out to those who knew what they were doing. This was a business expense I did not enjoy paying for; so I would watch these professional repairmen and ask plenty of questions. What I didn't learn by watching, I learned by reading, and eventually I learned to do most of the repairs myself. (I recommend the Reader's Digest *Complete Do-It-Yourself Manual*.)

Sweat equity essentially is hard work you do yourself to increase the value of the property. You could hire the repair work out to a professional, but that decision is based on whether you have adequate repair funds available. If you decide to hire a contractor, follow these guidelines: (1) Discuss the job you want done with at least two contractors and get written bids for the work. (2) Talk to your neighbors and ask them if they can recommend someone. Good craftsmen build their business on their reputation, so satisfied customers will be your best guide. (3) Get at least three references from the contractor and check them out. Call each reference and ask whether there were any problems; if there were, were they corrected? Also inquire into whether there were extra charges and whether the work was completed on time.

PAINTING THE INTERIOR

Latex paints are recommended for painting the interior because they are easy to apply, can be thinned and cleaned up with water, dry quickly, and have little or no odor. Flat latex paint is best for interior walls and ceilings. Semi-gloss or enamel finishes are preferred on woodwork, such as doors, window trim, and baseboards. Semi-gloss is also preferred on walls of bathrooms and kitchens because it will absorb more scrubbing and abuse than flat paints.

Dark colors tend to make rooms appear smaller, while light colors make rooms appear spacious and airy, and will more aptly suit most furniture schemes. Recommended is an off-white color like antique white or beige. If you keep all your rentals painted in one standard color, you'll work more efficiently, avoiding the expense and waste of partly filled paint cans of a variety of colors.

Careless painting wastes time and makes your investment look messy. Proper preparation is necessary to do a good quality job that will endure over the years. You can save money by purchasing your paint in five gallon cans instead of single gallons. Start by covering everything with plastic drop cloths to protect the furniture and floor. Next wash the walls and woodwork with soap and water. (Paint adheres better to a clean, non-glossy finish.) Fill all the cracks and holes by spackling. Let dry and then sand to a smooth finish. Remove all fixtures, electrical plates, and switch covers from surfaces to be painted. Also cover with masking tape such items as door knobs and glass not meant to be painted. Then, apply paint to the ceiling first, then the walls, and finish up with the trim and semi-gloss work.

PREVENTIVE MAINTENANCE

Owning and operating rental property can at times have its annoyances and headaches. Nevertheless, most of these nuisances can be overcome by keeping up with preventive maintenance and informing your tenants of certain guidelines they should follow.

Stopped-up drains are probably a renter or homeowner's biggest headache. The remedy is to install drain strainers (similar to a screen) in your bathtubs and bathroom sinks. This inexpensive device traps hair and large material before it can start collecting in your pipes. The most common cause of drain stoppage is children's toys blocking the drain. If you rent to people with children, inform them of the reason for the drain strainer and request that their children refrain from putting small toys in toilets and bathtubs. Bear in mind the old saying, "An ounce of prevention is worth a pound of cure."

SHOWING AND RENTING VACANT UNITS

This section is delegated to a step-by-step procedure of taking a vacant unit through all the necessary steps to fill it with a good, qualified, paying tenant. While your particular available unit might be the greatest rental in the city, a vacant house or apartment will remain unoccupied indefinitely if the public doesn't know it is available. On the other hand, if you rent the unit to an undesirable, non-paying deadbeat, you will soon wish the unit were vacant! The surest way to financial suicide, or at least a migraine headache, is to continually rent to flaky people who won't pay. There are enough qualified prospects to fill your vacant unit; all you have to do is advertise for them, and then properly qualify them.

Advertising

Prospecting for tenants is best accomplished through the vacancy signs and classified advertising in your local newspaper. Vacancy signs must be precise and to the point, qualifying the prospective tenant to a certain degree. For example, "Vacancy, 1-Bedroom, Adults Only," or "Vacancy, 2-Bedroom, Kids OK." By stating certain facts about the available unit, you will eliminate a lot of unqualified prospects who are looking for something you don't have. Your signs should be legible and large enough so they can easily be seen from a passing vehicle. Erect your vacancy signs on either side of your building, or post them on the lawn near the busiest street for maximum exposure.

Classified advertising should also be precise and qualifying in order to eliminate unnecessary calls from unqualified people. The four basic principles of good advertising are "AIDA" *ATTENTION:* Your headline should attract specific prospects. *INTEREST:* You should expand the headline and offer a benefit to the prospect that makes him read the rest of the ad. *DESIRE:* With good descriptive copy, make the prospect want what you have to offer. *ACTION:* Ask for action by making it easy for the prospect to respond to your offer.

ATTENTION . . . Could be a heading like "Newly Decorated," or "Large 3-Bedroom." The purpose of the attention heading is to get the reader to distinguish your ad from the numerous other ads in the same column. Another example would be "Free Rent for One Month." (This type of ad might be used in a rental market already oversupplied with available units. Free rent would definitely get more attention than the other ads in the same column.)

INTEREST . . . To develop interest one should offer a benefit like "2-fireplaces," or "Newly Carpeted," or "Great Ocean View" to entice the reader to finish reading the balance of your advertisement.

DESIRE . . . This will precisely describe what you have to offer. Like "2-Bedroom, Kids OK, $375," or "1-Bedroom, Adults Only, Pool, $350."

ACTION . . . Can be simply a phone number for the prospect to call and inquire.

Classified advertising is printed under specific headings so there is no need to duplicate information that is already available. In other words, it is not necessary to state that your apartment is unfurnished when your ad is running under the column "Unfurnished Apartments," or stating that your house is downtown when your ad is running under a column denoting specific areas in your city.

Begin your ad with the location, then the type of unit. For example:

NEAR DOWNTOWN . . . 2-bedroom, 1-bath, patio and
large fenced yard, kids and pets ok. $475.
Call 555-1212.

By beginning your ad with the location you qualify people right from the start. People look for rentals usually based on areas they want to live in. Anyone looking for a two bedroom in the downtown area will respond to this ad; anyone looking for a three bedroom in a different area will look elsewhere.

After a full description, including any particular features, close the ad with the amount of rent you're charging and a phone number to call. The amount of rent is important because you again qualify the prospect. If you're charging more for rent than the prospect can afford to pay, he won't bother to call.

The following was a sample advertisement that proved very effective. It ran in my local newspaper under the section Unfurnished Condominiums For Rent:

RENT WITH OPTION TO BUY . . . Spring Mt. & Jones,
3-Bedroom, 2-Bath, neat & clean, beautifully land-
scaped and decorated, w/tennis cts, pool & jacuzzi.
$595. Call 555-1212.

Showing the Vacant Unit

At this point your advertisement is running in the local paper and your vacancy signs are strategically located on the available unit. Now it is imperative that the vacant unit be ready to be shown, which means it should be neat and clean throughout. If by chance you are renting an occupied unit that the occupants will be moving out of shortly, then inform the occupants of your intentions. Request that they keep the unit tidy so that you can show the unit to prospects.

While you're showing the unit, begin pointing out features of the unit, such as storage, cabinets, view, and so on. Do not bring up what you might consider to be negative, because what may be a negative aspect to some may not be to others. Furthermore, you should know the exact square footage of the available unit.

The prospects, if they are interested in the unit, will usually begin by asking questions concerning schools (What are they? What are their reputations?), transportation (Do you know the bus schedules?), shopping, and so on—questions which you should be prepared to answer. If you do not know about the schools in the area, for example, find out what they are.

Renting the Unit

At this point your prospective tenants have seen the unit and have decided to rent it. What do you do now? First, get as much of a deposit as you can and *do not accept a check for a deposit.* Your prospects could order a stop-payment on the check once they left the premises, and you would be stuck with a worthless check. Accept only cash or a money order for the deposit, and make sure it's for at least $100 or more. Anything less could entice your prospects into not upholding their obligation should they find something they preferred before moving into your rental.

After receiving the deposit and giving your prospects a receipt, have them complete the Rental Application Form. (See Rental Application Form in Forms Section following this chapter.) Be sure your prospects fill out the application completely, because you will use this information later to determine whether you will accept them as tenants. Once they have completed the application, check for omissions, and if there are none, notify your tenants that you will phone them once you make a decision on their application.

QUALIFYING THE PROSPECTIVE TENANT

From the Rental Application Form you now have to determine whether it would be wise to accept your new applicants as tenants. Essentially what you are looking for is someone who will take reasonably good care of the premises, pay their rent on time, and not be a nuisance. Bear in mind that you are about to develop a long-term business relationship with these people, and you do not need the headaches associated with people who won't, or don't, have the capability to pay their rent on time. Once a tenant has gained possession of your rental unit and decides not to pay his rent and you want him removed, you must do it by "due process of law." Lawful actions to evict a deadbeat will only bring a judgment for rent monies, court costs, and moving fees. Cases that go to court will undoubtedly require 30 days or more to remedy. The costs involved, plus additional loss of rent, can be very expensive to an owner when this professional deadbeat moves in to your property.

The best way to avoid this catastrophic situation is to check on your prospect's history-of-paying habits. Telephone a local credit agency and find out what they require to do a credit check for you. If they have no credit, then inquire into their rent-paying habits with the past two landlords. Occasionally, I will ask prospective tenants if I can see their credit cards. If in fact they have active Visa or Master-Card accounts, that is usually a sign of good credit, which allows me not to check their credit any further. Be sure you check the expiration date when you're inspecting credit cards.

Your next concern is whether your future tenants will properly care for your investment while they're living in it? About the only way you can determine that is by calling the previous landlord and inquiring into their living habits. Incidentally, through my past

20 years of landlording experience, I have observed certain habits of human nature which may assist novice landlords. It has been my experience that people who take good care of their vehicle will in most cases, take good care of the home they live in. Conversely, people who drive a dirty, ill-maintained car in almost every case have dirty and messy homes and won't take very good care of your property. This observation will also usually hold true for kids. If the children of the family are reasonably well dressed in clean clothes it would be a good assumption on your part that the parents will also care for other things, such as your investment. So, when your prospective tenants arrive at your available unit, check out the condition of the car and the children, if any. Later, if you have any doubts about renting to them, let your observations assist in making your decision.

Finally, it is necessary to financially qualify your prospects on their ability to pay the rent. The guidelines for rent qualification are as follows: The monthly rent should not exceed 25 percent of the tenant's gross monthly income. However, if he has no consumer debt (i.e., car loans and credit card payments), then he can afford up to 33 percent of his gross monthly income. Spouse income can be included, but not overtime pay. For example, if your prospect grosses $2,000 per month and has certain consumer debt, then he really cannot afford to pay more than $500 per month in rent ($2,000 × 25 %). If he has no consumer debt, then he could afford one-third of $2,000, or $667 per month in rent.

RENTING CONSIDERATIONS

Generally speaking, the more at risk you are, the more you should require in deposits. You are more at risk when the family you rent to has children or pets, such as dogs and cats. Usually, the security deposit on an unfurnished home can be from 75 to 100 percent of the first month's rent. This amount can be adjusted upwards for each child or pet in the family. A security deposit is a refundable deposit. Any damage done by the tenants, if any, is deducted from the deposit, then sent to them within 30 days from move-out.

Another necessary deposit is the nonrefundable cleaning deposit. (Note that certain states prohibit nonrefundable cleaning deposits, therefore check your local statutes regarding this matter.) The cleaning deposit is normally priced in the range of $75 to $125, depending on the size and value of the rental. Before your tenants move in, be sure to inform them that both the security and cleaning deposits cannot be applied to the last month's rent when they vacate the premises, and that the security deposit will be held until after the unit is vacated with proper notice and in reasonably good condition.

Separate deposits should be required for certain keys, such as key cards (for parking in secured condominium complexes and for tennis courts, etc.). Usually $10 is adequate for keys and $25 each for a key card.

THE MOVE-IN

Before your tenants move in and take over residency of your rental unit, certain items have to be taken care of. All monies owed to you have to be paid in advance in cash. This includes the first month's rent (or first and last if it's a long-term lease), and all deposits, including security, cleaning, and key deposits. Be sure the rental agreement is signed and that there is one copy available for the tenant. Also be sure the tenant has one set of keys, plus information on who to call for the turn-on of all utilities. Finally, inform them that you expect the rent to be paid on time, that there is a three-day grace period, but after that a late fee will be charged. (See lease provisions in Forms Section later in this chapter.)

RENT COLLECTION

Remember, your investment in real estate is purely a money-making enterprise, not a downtown mission run on charity. Investors who yield to delinquent or nonpaying deadbeats are courting financial disaster. Therefore, be firm with your collection policies and inform your new tenants at the time of move-in what you expect of them. However, you can be flexible. All rents do not have to be paid on the first day of the month. Under certain circumstances, some people might receive their paychecks on the tenth of the month or the fifteenth. If this is the case, make their rent due on a date to coincide with their payday.

After all move-in fees have been paid in cash, you can then have a policy of accepting checks for the monthly rent payments. This policy is fine, unless you receive a bad check, and once you do, then your policy should be to accept only cash or money orders from that individual from that point on. Check bouncers are a habitual bunch. If you continue to accept checks after one has bounced, you can be assured that more rubber checks will eventually bounce through your bank account.

Rent checks should be mailed directly to an address of your choice. Once a tenant has established a good payment history with you, more lenient allowances can be made when unforseen circumstances occur, such as the loss of employment, illness, or death in the family. Whatever the case, definite commitments must be made as to when the debt will be paid and must be immediately followed up on if not.

Resident Manager—Rent-Collection Policy

The following are recommended procedures in the event you have a resident manager living on the premises of your multi-unit building. Rent collection should always be in the form of checks or money orders. Absolutely no cash should be accepted. (An exception can be made in the case of emergency or when someone is extremely late in paying the rent.) By having a policy of only accepting checks or money orders, you will eliminate the temptation of the resident manager to borrow small amounts of cash and you will alleviate the risk of the rent monies being stolen.

Each month's rent receipts can be deposited by the resident manager. To do this, order a rubber stamp from the printer, then the manager can stamp the back of the rent checks (For Deposit Only . . .), then deposit them in your bank account.

Receipt of rent is occasionally requested by the tenant. Therefore, it is necessary to furnish the manager with a receipt pad in triplicate. One copy of a rent receipt can then be available for the tenant, one for the manager, and one copy for the owner's records.

Delinquent Sheet

It is essentially a list of overdue tenants.

The resident manager uses the delinquent sheet in rent collection. Assume that all the rents of a particular building are due on the first day of the month. The delinquent sheet has the name of each tenant on it, with a comment section next to the tenant's name so the manager can make notes. As each tenant pays the rent, the name is crossed off the list. Let's say Mrs. Jones in apartment 102 tells the manager that she will pay the rent on the third. The manager would then make a note to that effect on the delinquent list. If a three-day notice was issued, or if an eviction notice was issued to a tenant, this would also be noted. The delinquent sheet is a tool used in record keeping that allows an immediate report on the current rent status.

Eviction Procedure (Nonpayment of Rent)

The following procedure is common in most states for the lawful eviction of a tenant for nonpayment of rent:

1. The tenant in default is served with a Three-Day Notice to Pay Rent or Quit the Premises. The person serving the notice should be the marshal, not the landlord, owner, or resident manager, in order to insure proper legal procedure.

2. An Unlawful Detainer is filed with the municipal court clerk, and a Summons is issued.

3. The tenant is served with a Summons and a Complaint.

4. The tenant has the legal right to file against the Complaint, pleading his case. In that event a trial is held.

5. The default of tenant is taken and given to the owner.

6. The court issues a Writ of Possession.

7. The marshal receives the Writ of Possession.

8. The marshal evicts the tenant.

CHOOSING THE RESIDENT MANAGER

Whether you own a fourplex, 20 units, or one building with 50 units or more, it will be necessary to have a resident manager permanently on the premises. When the owner has a competent manager on the property, he is relieved of many time-consuming operations and responsibilities.

The ideal resident manager team is a husband and wife, with the wife handling the management responsibilities and the husband doing the maintenance. Ideally, the husband would be working a full-time job elsewhere while the wife would be free to manage your building. The following are the chief qualities you should look for in a management team, listed in their order of importance:

1. Honesty

2. Eagerness and willingness to do the job properly.

3. Ability to accept responsibility.

4. Husband that is handy at minor repairs.

5. A wife with a pleasant personality and a willingness to stay at home and assist in the overall operation of the property.

6. Experience.

It is primarily the manager's responsibility to collect rent, show vacancies, and keep the common grounds clean. The husband can handle minor repair work and mow the lawn. Then you can eliminate the need to always call a professional repair person or hire a lawn maintenance service.

It is very important that the wife, as resident manager, be on the job to show vacancies and keep order around the building. A wife that is overly active outside the home having numerous social commitments is not a good prospect, while the domestic housewife having children is, as she tends to be at home more.

What you pay the husband and wife management team depends on the size of the building being managed. Managing a 20-unit building typically would be free rent. For a smaller building, like a fourplex or sixplex, a 25 percent reduction in rental rate would be typical. Buildings larger than 20 units usually involve free rent plus a cash salary. For competitive salaries look in your local newspaper in the classified section under the column "Couples Wanted."

Supervising the Resident Manager

Duties of the resident manager must be fully explained at the beginning of the owner-employee relationship. Be sure the manager knows exactly what is expected of them. Remember, the more responsibility you as owner can delegate to the manager, the more time you will have to pursue other matters.

Monthly reports submitted to the owner are necessary for efficient accounting and ready reference. These reports include a summary of rents (income) collected, a delinquency sheet, and bank deposits made (optional, depending on whether it is the manager or the owner who makes the deposit).

Each entry on the summary of rents (income) collected should include apartment number, rent paid date and due date, amount paid, and type of income (rent, cleaning fee, key deposit, or security deposit). One copy of the rent receipt is also kept on file by the manager, and the tenant receives the third copy, if requested.

Major expenditures, such as replacing carpet or a hot water heater, should be billed directly to the owner. In fact, it will be helpful if the owner can establish charge accounts with various suppliers. This will reduce the temptation of the manager to pad expense bills or receive kickbacks from salespeople.

Once you have a qualified and responsible management team operating your building, you'll find that an occasional monthly supervisory visit is all that is required of the owner's time. Major decisions, such as expensive repairs or recarpeting can be accomplished on such visits. In addition, the owner can pick up and make an inspection of the premises during these visits. Thus, the joys of landlording can be enriched by a responsible manager, thereby avoiding the headaches and hassles many amateur owners experience through slipshod management practices.

BUDGETING

The successful operation of a multi-unit building will ultimately depend on a carefully planned budget, then sticking to it without exception. The budget is basically financial planning for the upcoming years. Projections of all income and expenses are made so that an overall view of the building's financial well-being can be viewed. If owners do not properly plan income and expenses, the ultimate disaster of financial suicide is inevitable. Allocations for certain replacement items over the years have to be budgeted and paid for when they need replacing. What happens when owners do not plan properly is deferred maintenance. That, in turn, causes vacancies, which, in turn, causes loss of income and further deferred maintenance and eventual loss in value.

Good budgeting not only encompasses the planning of income and expenses but also the future replacement of capital items, such as carpeting, roofs, pool equipment, and furniture. These items are very costly, but through properly planned budgets, they can easily be replaced when needed. Thus, a contingency fund should be set aside and held in reserve to replace these items when needed. For example, carpeting usually has to be replaced every seven years, on average. New carpeting in today's market for a one-bedroom apartment will cost about $700 and will last for seven years. Therefore, $100 per year per apartment (about $8 per month) should be set aside in a contingency fund to replace carpeting. Similarly, a replacement reserve fund must be set up for items such as draperies, roofing, furniture, and appliances.

The best way to budget these items is to estimate total outlay for all future capital expenditures, maintaining the fund for each item in a savings account to use when the money is required. For example, you determine that the cost of a new roof is $1,200, and it will last for 20 years. Therefore, divide the total cost by the total number of months and the result is the amount that should be budgeted each month ($1,200 ÷ 240 months = $5 per month allocation for a replacement reserve for roofing).

Expense items, such as property taxes and hazard insurance, also have to be budgeted. (Note: Taxes and insurance frequently are paid out of an impound account which is already part of your monthly payment.) If this is the case, it won't be necessary for you to pay separately the taxes and insurance premium because the holder of the first mortgage will pay these from the impound account. If the first note holder is not paying the taxes and insurance, then it will be necessary for you to arrange these items in your budget. Property taxes are projected at $\frac{1}{12}$ of the annual tax bill per month. Be sure to allow for a future increase by the assessor. Hazard insurance is likewise $\frac{1}{12}$ of the annual insurance premium.

As a rule of thumb, 5 percent of gross collected rents is usually an adequate amount to be budgeted for replacement reserves. However, this amount would have to be increased if your building had additional equipment, such as an elevator, heated pool or jacuzzi.

KEEPING RECORDS

Proper record-keeping procedures are necessary so the information will be accessible when needed, especially when income tax time arrives or in the event the IRS decides to make an untimely audit. Keeping records can be accomplished very simply when your investments are single-family homes. All you need is a separate 8.5" × 11" manila envelope for each home, properly labeled, while keeping all records and expense items inside the envelope. All income collected can be noted on the outside of the envelope, along with addresses of note holders, balance owing on the notes, and initial cost of the property. At the end of each year, a new envelope can be started for the upcoming year.

Multi-unit buildings require a little more elaborate record-keeping systems, with a separate set of records being required for each building. Make up file folders and label them "General Records," "Tenant Records," and "Receipts and Expenses." In the general records folder retain such information as escrow papers, insurance policies, taxes, notes, and deeds. In the tenant record folder, maintain all rental applications, rental agreements, and any other data pertaining to your tenants. All tenant information should be kept for credit rating purposes and landlord inquiries for at least one year after tenants move out. In the receipt folder, retain all paid receipts for all expenses related to the building and a copy of all rent receipts. Later the expense items can be arranged chronologically for tax purposes. At the end of the tax year, this envelope should be stored separately for at least five years, in case the IRS decides to audit.

Cardex

A tenant record, or cardex, is a 5.5″ × 8″ card used by the owner or manager. Whenever a tenant makes payment, it is recorded on the cardex. (See sample of cardex in forms section.) A separate cardex is maintained on each rental unit. It is a ready reference of all monies paid and due, plus other important tenant information.

Journal of Income and Expenses

A separate journal is required for each multi-unit building for which you will post all relevant income and expense data monthly. It includes sections on income, expenses, loans, and depreciation, and it allows you ready access to all current data relating to income and expense. The first section denotes rental and laundry income for each unit for the entire year, and the second section is for posting expenses. All those receipts you have been keeping in a file folder are recorded here monthly. Anything you do not have receipts for can be recorded from your checking account record. Examples of the Monthly Income and Expense and Payment Record follow on the next two pages.

Once you have completed an entire page on the Expense and Payment Record, total each column and bring the balance forward to the next sheet, then start posting your latest entries. After you have posted your last expenditure for the year, total the last sheet and you'll have your annual expenses for each category of your building.

Monthly Income Record   Page # _____
Address _____
Year _____

Unit	Jan	Feb	Mar	Apr	May	Jun	Jul	Aug	Sep	Oct	Nov	Dec
1	400	400	400	400	400							
2	390	390	390	390	390							
3	425	425	425	425	425							
4	275	275	275	275	275							
5	415	415	415	415	415							
6	460	460	460	460	460							
7												
8												
Tot.	2365	2365	2365	2365	2365							

Expense and Payment Record

Address _____ Year _____ Page # _____

Date	Paid To	Paid For	Total Paid	Mortgage Principal	Mortgage Interest	Tax	Ins	Mgt	Repairs & Maint.
1. 1/1	bank	1st mort	760	122.80	427.20	120	90		
2. 1/1	Smith	2nd	125	92.40	32.60				
3. 1/3	hdwr.	pts.	9.60						
4. 1/7	water	water	56.71						
5. 1/8	muni ct	evict	21						
6. 2/1	bank	1st mort	760	124.06	425.94	120	90		
7.									

Be careful not to post on your expense record such capital items as carpeting or a new roof. These are depreciable items, not expenses.

Depreciation Records

Depreciable items are property or equipment having an extended useful life and considered to be improvements to the property. Some examples are: Carpeting, elevators, new linoleum, roof replacement, swimming pool. Each of these items must be depreciated on a separate depreciation record form. (See depreciation methods in the tax chapter.)

The following is a depreciation record used for the building itself (a similar depreciation record can be used for capital improvements):

Location and description of capital improvement:
3750 Raymond, LA, CA. A 19-unit apartment building

Date acquired:	Jan. 1967
New or Used:	Used
Cost or value:	$220,000
Land value:	40,000
Salvage value:	0
Depreciable Basis:	$180,000
Method of depreciation:	125% declining balance
Useful life:	20 years

	Year	Prior Deprec.	Deprec. Balance	% Year Held	Deprec. this yr.
1.	1967	0	180,000	100	11,250
2.	1968	11,250	168,750	100	10,547
3.	1969	10.547	158,203	100	9.888
4.					

Annual Statement of Income

This statement brings together all relative income and expense for the year and shows the net profit or loss. Notice how depreciation, not an out-of-pocket expense, is deducted last for tax purposes. (This is the actual "tax-shelter" benefit of owning income-producing real estate.) The final bottom line is the net profit or loss given to the Internal Revenue Service.

POINTS TO REMEMBER

Property management can be a truly rewarding experience or it can be a burdensome daily chore. I have endeavored to offer you a con-

Annual Statement of Income Example
  Location: 3750 Raymond, LA, CA.   Year: 1968

Income		
Rent	$28,471	
Other (laundry)	629	
Total Income	29,100	$29,100
Expenses		
Interest	8,410	
Taxes	4,800	
Utilities	1,812	
Service, repairs	321	
Pest control	120	
Insurance	850	
Management	1,800	
Total Expenses	18,113	18,113
Net Income (before Depreciation)		10,987
Less depreciation		− 11,250
Net Income (or loss) for tax purposes		($263)

cise, yet thorough, guide for total property management to assist you at making decisions and to help you avoid costly pitfalls. Foremost among these guidelines is properly screening your prospective tenants, thereby helping to insure you will have good-paying tenants who will properly care for your investment. And don't forget the importance of the "no-hassle" clause written into your rental agreement. This will eliminate 90 percent of the late-night phone calls by your tenants requesting repairs. These simple procedures will help to make your investment a truly efficient, successful, and profitable experience.

11 FORMS SECTION

The following forms in this section are for your use as you see fit, including duplication of each page on any type of photocopy equipment.

APPLICATION TO RENT

Investment in real estate is essentially a money-making enterprise, not a downtown mission run on charity. You have a lot invested, both in effort and money, so why in the world would you rent to a non-paying deadbeat or a malicious tenant? Yet, time after time, inexperienced property owners rent out their beloved properties without taking the time to properly qualify prospective tenants. Remember, you are essentially loaning your property to someone for his use for a considerable period of time. A business relationship is about to develop, and if you rent to someone who habitually pays late and isn't capable of taking reasonably good care of your property, you're in for plenty of trouble.

You can overcome most of the problems frequently encountered by novice landlords by properly qualifying your prospective renters. Good-paying tenants who will take good care of your property are a valuable asset. Here is some sound advice to assist you in judging whether or not your prospective tenants have the good character and capability of meeting the terms of your rental agreement.

After your prospect has completed filling out the rental application, review it carefully. Make sure everything is legible and complete. Make sure the name is correct, because later on if Jim Jones skips the premises, he will be easier to trace with his complete name of James Anthony Jones. If more than one person will occupy the premises, get names of all the adults and find out who is responsible for rent payments.

Employment information is also very important. You definitely want to qualify the prospect on his ability to pay rent. As a general rule of thumb, a range of 25 percent to 33 percent of gross monthly income can safely be paid in rent. Lenders use a similar formula when making loans wherein they will allow 25 percent of gross income to be paid in rent. If there were some other debt obligations, such as credit cards, car payments, and so on, then only a maximum of 25 percent could be applied toward rent; if there were none, then 33 percent of gross monthly income could be applied to rent payments.

If your prospect qualifies by his salary, then at a more appropriate time you should verify employment. A simple phone call to the employer is sufficient.

Credit References
This information will be supplied to a local credit bureau, if it is necessary. What I usually do is, after the prospect has completed the rental application, I ask to see his credit cards. If, in fact, he has active, up-to-date cards (which have not expired), that satisfies any doubts I may have about his credit worthiness. Just the fact that he has acquired Visa, MasterCard, or Sears credit cards is usually a good indication of credit-worthiness. One final credit check would be to call either his last, or second-from-last landlord and inquire into his character and rent-paying habits.

Spouse/Roommate (Part of Rental Application)
You will have added protection by having the spouse or roommate sign all the documents of the Rental Agreement. This way both parties are jointly responsible, and it may be easier to locate one of the tenants if the other skips.

Discrimination Laws
As a landlord you cannot, according to the law, refuse to rent to people because of their race, creed, color, national origin, sex, or marital status. This doesn't mean, however, that you are obligated to rent to anyone just because they have a fistful of money. In particular for a multi-unit building, you should have certain standards to induce harmony in your building. For example, single adults prefer living in a building where other singles live. Likewise, families with children usually prefer to live in complexes which cater to other families. Similarly, senior citizens prefer to live where they're not annoyed by barking dogs and children at play. Therefore, set certain standards if you own multi-unit buildings and don't try and mix the elderly with the young, or singles with families.

APPLICATION TO RENT

	Home	Work

Name _____ Phone _____ Phone _____

Spouse/Roomate Name _____ Work Ph. _____

Unit to be occupied by _____ Adults and ____ Children and ____ Pets

Present Address _____ City _____ State _____ Zip _____

Current Landlord/Mgr's Name _____ Phone _____

Why are you leaving? _____

Previous Address _____ City _____ State _____ Zip _____

Landlord/Mgr's Name _____ Phone _____

Applicant's Birth Date _____ Soc. Sec. # _____ Driv. Lic. _____

Applicant's Employer_____ Position _____ How long _____

Applicant's Employer's Address _____ Gross monthly pay _____

Spouse/Roomate's Employer _____ Gross monthly pay _____

Credit References: Bank _____ Account # _____ Type _____

Other Active Reference _____ Account # _____

Spouse/Roomate Credit Ref. _____ Account # _____

In an emergency contact: _____ Phone _____

Address _____ City _____ State _____ Zip _____

List all motor vehicles, including RV's, to be kept at the dwelling unit. Include make, model, year, and license plate # for each.

Vehicle #1 _____ Vehicle #2 _____

License _____ License _____

Vehicle #3 _____

License _____

I (we) declare that the above information is correct and I (we) give my (our) permission for any reporting agency to release my credit file to undersigned landlord solely for the purposes of entering into a rental agreement. I (we) further authorize the Landlord or his agent to verify the above information including but not limited to contacting creditors, both listed herein or not, and present or former landlords.

Dated _____, 19 ____   Applicant _____

                                      Applicant _____

INVENTORY OF FURNISHINGS

This form should accompany the lease for each individual unit. It essentially identifies items such as the refrigerator, stove, couch, etc., and denotes its current condition. Later in a lawsuit the land-lord can claim any damage, excluding reasonable wear and tear, against the security/cleaning deposits. The tenants, on the other hand, may counter that the damage was there prior to move-in. Except in cases of gross and negligent damage, a defense of "the damage was there before we moved in" is difficult to overcome unless proper documentation is provided.

At the time of move-in, have the tenants go through the unit room by room with you. Have the tenants fill out the inventory and mark any comments and return the form to you. If comments cannot be made in the space provided, have your tenants make any additional comments on the reverse side of this form and note "See reverse side."

INVENTORY OF FURNISHINGS

Rental unit address _____

Tenant _____ Inventory date _____, 19 _____

_____

Room	Item	Comments	Condition at Move-out

Tenant agrees that the above information is an accurate inventory and description and assumes responsibility for these items in the dwelling unit as of _____, 19 _____.

Move-in		Move-out	
_____ Date _____		_____ Date _____	
_____ Date _____		_____ Date _____	

CARDEX

A tenant record, or cardex, is a 5.5" × 8" card used by the owner or manager. It is a ready reference of all monies paid and due, plus other important tenant information, since every payment, is recorded on the cardex. See sample of Cardex on page 145.

NOTICE OF CHANGE IN TERMS
OF RENTAL AGREEMENT

This form is used to change the rental rate. Usually, 30 days are required for a suitable notice before increasing the rental rate. Specific rental rates are found in the initial rental agreement. However, once the original term of the agreement expires, the landlord can, at his option, increase the rental rate.

REMINDERS TO PAY RENT

Delinquency by your tenants should not be tolerated. Good landlords should predictably react immediately to non-payment of rent when it is due. Slow-paying tenants usually will react to this predictability and make the rent a high priority on their list of payments. Normally there is a three-day grace period after the rent due date. If the rent is

NOTICE OF CHANGE IN TERMS OF RENTAL AGREEMENT

Date _____

To _____, Tenant in possession of _____
_____.

[ ] Certified mail
[ ] Hand delivered
[ ] Regular mail

You are hereby notified that the terms of tenancy under which you occupy the above address are to be changed as follows:

Effective _____, 19 _____, your rent will be increased by $ _____ per month for a total of $ _____ each month.

_____
Landlord/Agent

Sample of Cardex

Address: _____

KEY SIGNATURE _____

Orig. Move-In Date _____
Lease Dated _____ Exp. _____
Tenant Tel. No. _____

DEPOSIT

RENT

Date Due	Date Paid	Receipt Number	Paid To Noon	Amount Paid	Security Deposit	Cleaning Fee	Key Deposit #	Base Rent	Refrig-erator	Furniture	Parking	Month to Month	Additional Occupancy	Other Fireplace & Dishwasher	Air Conditioner	Utilities		Total Rent	Balance Due

BLDG. # _____ APT. _____ TYPE _____ FL. PL. _____ CLR. _____ NAME _____

Date Due

THREE-DAY REMINDER TO PAY RENT

To _____   Date _____

_____

Just a reminder that your rent was past due on _____. According to the terms of your Rental Agreement, rent more than _____ days past due requires a late charge payment of $ _____. We would appreciate your prompt payment.

Thank you,

_____

Landlord/Agent

FIVE-DAY REMINDER TO PAY RENT

To _____   Date _____

_____

Your rent is now past due as of _____. As of this date, the past-due rent and late charges total $ _____.

You must settle this account or our legal options will have to be considered. Therefore please act to remedy this matter immediately.

Thank you,

_____

Landlord/Agent

not received within three days of due date, action has to be taken. Collection experts agree that a first notice be sent within five days of the due date and a second notice after seven days. In the event your slow-paying tenant has a history of continued delinquency, a Three-Day Notice To Pay or Quit the Premises could be used in favor of the second notice.

NOTICE TO PAY RENT
OR QUIT THE PREMISES

This form is the three-day pay or quit initiated by the landlord and issued to the tenant in default. Essentially, the tenant has three days from date of this notice to pay all monies in default or move out of the premises. This form is to be issued to the tenant only after the land-

NOTICE TO PAY RENT OR QUIT THE PREMISES

To _____   Date _____

_____   [ ] Delivered by Marshal

[ ] Certified mail #_____

[ ] Hand delivered

You are hereby notified that the rent for the period _____, 19 _____,
to _____, 19 _____, is now past due. As of this date, the total sum
owing including late charges is $ _____. Unless this sum is received
within three days of this dated notice, you will be required to vacate and sur-
render the premises.

If it becomes necessary to proceed with legal action for the non-payment of
rent or to obtain possession of the premises, as per the terms of the Rental
Agreement, you will be liable for recovery of our reasonable attorney fees and
expenses. You will also be liable for any additional rent for the time you are
in possession of the premises.

_____

Landlord/Agent

lord has attempted to procure the amount owed through other means,
such as the three- and five-day reminder notices. Note: Caution should
be taken in this matter of the Pay or Quit Notice because laws vary
substantially on this matter throughout the country. This particular
form may not conform to the laws in some states where new landlord/
tenant statutes have been enacted. If this is the case, the landlord
should seek the appropriate form at a reputable legal stationary store
or consult with an attorney.

NOTICE OF ABANDONED PROPERTY

Abandoned personal property, which the tenant left behind for whatever reason (which in most cases is of little or no value) has to be
disposed of according to the prevailing laws within your particular
state. If you carelessly dispose of abandoned property, whether it has
value or not, you could leave yourself open to a legal suit or a malicious extenant seeking revenge.

Abandoned-property statutes can vary substantially from state to
state. Junked or abandoned cars frequently are left behind also but are
treated differently. If you should be faced with an old junker on your
vacated property, it is best to call your local Department of Motor
Vehicles and find out the best way to dispose of it. Junk yards are

usually not allowed to accept vehicles unless the car has a valid signed-off certificate of title.

Most states do require proof that an effort was in fact made to contact the rightful owner of the property. Therefore, in most cases, this notice should be sufficient and should be sent to the rightful owner of the abandoned property at his last known address. Caution: If there is obvious substantial value to the property in question, or if you are not familiar with local statutes regarding this matter, please consult with a qualified attorney.

NOTICE OF ABANDONED PROPERTY

To _____   Date _____

Address _____

When you vacated the rented unit located at _____
you left the following described property on the premises: _____

_____

_____.

You are hereby informed that unless you claim and remove the above-described property before _____, 19 _____, it will be thrown away, given to charity, or sold in a manner prescribed by law. If sold, the proceeds will be used to cover the cost of the sale, then to cover any sums due, and any remaining balance will be forwarded to you.

Please take care of this matter immediately.

_____

Landlord/Agent

_____

RENTAL-AGREEMENT RESIDENTIAL LEASE

1. This Lease made this _____ day of _____, 19 _____, by and between _____,
hereinafter called Landlord, and _____,
hereinafter called Tenant.

2. *Description:* Witnesseth, the Landlord, in consideration of the rents to be paid and the covenants and agreements to be performed by the Tenant, does hereby lease unto the Tenant the following described premises located thereon situated in the City of _____, County of _____,
State of _____, commonly known as _____

_____.

3. *Terms:* For the term of _____ (months/years) commencing on _____, 19 _____, and ending on _____
_____, 19 _____.

4. *Rent*: Tenant shall pay Landlord, as rent for said premises, the sum of _____ dollars ($ _____) per month payable in advance on the first day of each month during the term hereof at Landlord's address above or said other place as Landlord may hereafter designate in writing. Tenant agrees to pay a $25 late fee if rent is not paid within five days of due date.

5. *Security Deposit*: Landlord herewith acknowledges the receipt of _____ _____ dollars ($ _____), which he is to retain as security for the faithful performance of the provisions of this Lease. If Tenant fails to pay rent, or defaults with respect to any provision of this Lease, Landlord may use the security deposit to cure the default or compensate Landlord for all damages sustained by Landlord. Tenant shall immediately on demand reimburse Landlord the sum equal to that portion of security deposit expended by Landlord so as to maintain the security deposit in the sum initially deposited with Landlord. If Tenant performs all obligations under this Lease, the security deposit, or that portion thereof that was not previously applied by Landlord, shall be returned to Tenant within 21 days after the expiration of this Lease, or after Tenant has vacated the premises.

6. *Possession*: It is understood that if the Tenant shall be unable to enter into and occupy the premises hereby leased at the time above provided, by reason of the said premises not being ready for occupancy, or by reason of holding over of any previous occupancy of said premises, the Landlord shall not be liable in damage to the Tenant therefore, but during the period the Tenant shall be unable to occupy said premises as hereinbefore provided, the rental therefore shall be abated and the Landlord is to be the sole judge as to when the premises are ready for occupancy.

7. *Use*: Tenant agrees that said premises during the term of this Lease shall be used and occupied by _____ adults and _____ children, and _____ animals, and for no purpose whatsoever other than a residence, without the written consent of the Landlord, and that Tenant will not use the premises for any purpose in violation of any law, municipal ordinance, or regulation, and at any breach of this agreement the Landlord may at his option terminate this Lease and re-enter and repossess the leased premises.

8. *Utilities*: Tenant will pay for all charges for all water supplied to the premises and pay for all gas, heat, electricity, and other services supplied to the premises, except as herein provided: _____.

9. *Repairs and Maintenance*: The Landlord shall at his expense, except for the first $100 in cost which the Tenant pays, keep and maintain the exterior walls, roof, electrical wiring, heating and air-conditioning system, water heater, built-in appliances, and water lines in good condition and repair, except where damage has been caused by negligence or abuse of the Tenant, in which case Tenant shall repair same at his sole expense.

Tenant hereby agrees that the premises are now in good condition and shall at his sole expense maintain the premises and appurtenances in the manner in which they were received, reasonable wear and tear excepted.

The _____ agrees to maintian landscaping and swimming pool (if any). Tenant agrees to adequately water landscaping.

10. *Alterations and Additions*: The Tenant shall not make any alterations, additions, or improvements to said premises without the Landlord's written consent. All alterations, additions, or improvements made by either of the parties hereto upon the premises, except movable furniture, shall be the property of the Landlord and shall remain upon and be surrendered with the premises at the termination of this Lease.

11. *Assignment*: The Tenant will not assign or transfer this lease or sublet said premises without the written consent of the Landlord.

12. *Default*: If the Tenant shall abandon or vacate said premises before the end of the term of this lease, or if default shall be made by the tenant in the payment of said rent or any part hereof, or if the Tenant shall fail to perform any of the Tenant's agreements in this lease, then and in each and every instance of such abandonment or default, the Tenant's right to enter said premises shall be suspended, and the Landlord may at his option enter said premises and remove and exclude the Tenant from said premises.

13. *Entry by Landlord*: Tenant shall allow the Landlord or his agents to enter the premises at all reasonable times and upon reasonable notice for the purpose of inspecting or maintaining the premises or to show it to prospective tenants or purchasers.

14. *Attorney's fees*: The Tenant agrees to pay all costs, expenses, and reasonable attorney's fees including obtaining advice of counsel incurred by Landlord in enforcing by legal action or otherwise any of Landlord's rights under this lease or under any law of this state.

15. *Holding Over*: If Tenant, with the Landlord's consent, remains in possession of the premises after expiration of the term of this lease, such possession will be deemed a month-to-month tenancy at a rental equal to the last monthly rental, and upon all the provisions of this lease applicable to such a month-to-month tenancy.

The parties hereto have executed this Lease on the date first above written.

Landlord	Tenant
By: _____	By: _____
	By: _____

PERSONAL FINANCIAL STATEMENT
(MONTHLY INCOME AND EXPENSES)

MONTHLY INCOME:
 Gross wages   _____
 Rental income   _____
  Property "A"   _____
  Property "B"   _____
 Interest income   _____
 Mortgage income   _____
 Other income   _____
TOTAL MONTHLY INCOME: ============

MONTHLY EXPENSES:
  Rent   _____
  Real estate loans   _____
    Property "A"   _____
    Property "B"   _____
  Vehicle loan   _____
  Furniture   _____
  Personal loans   _____
  Alimony or child support   _____
  Other   _____
TOTAL MONTHLY EXPENSES: ═══════════

BALANCE SHEET

ASSETS:
  Cash on hand   _____
  Cash in bank   _____
  Car (vehicle)   _____
  Life insurance (cash value)   _____
  Real estate: _____
    Property "A"   _____
    Property "B"   _____
  Stocks and bonds   _____
  Mortgages (owed to you)   _____
  Accounts receivable   _____
  Household furniture   _____
  Other personal property   _____
TOTAL ASSETS: ═══════════

LIABILITIES:
  Personal loans   _____
  Vehicle   _____
  Total real estate indebtedness   _____
  Other (furniture, etc.)   _____
TOTAL LIABILITIES: ═══════════

TOTAL NET WORTH: ═══════════

12 SELLING YOUR PROPERTY

Throughout the U.S.A. two-thirds of residential real estate is sold using the services of a broker (the remainder is sold by individual owners). The broker's fee for selling your home is usually 6 percent of the selling price. In return, the broker will assist you in determining the right selling price, show the home to prospective buyers, and list it with the Multiple Listing Service. Listing with the MLS substantially expands the market for potential buyers, because brokers and agents from other offices are made aware of your listing through the MLS, and they likewise inform their buyers of your available property.

Besides showing the property, the listing agent is also helpful at closing the sale. In many cases the broker can act as the liaison between you and the buyer, working out any difficulties that may arise.

However, should you decide to save the sales commission and sell the property yourself, the contents of this chapter explain the necessary steps to accomplish this. Keep in mind that, on average, it takes 87 days to sell a home. This shows that it is by no means an easy task. Much preparation is required to do the job right, so, if you're prepared to invest the time and effort necessary to sell your own property and save the 6 percent commission, go right ahead. The following material is a step-by-step guide to accomplishing this.

TIMING THE SALE

Traditionally there are good times during the year to sell residential property, and good times as well to buy. Good times to sell are during the spring and fall, primarily because it is the time most buyers are looking for property, especially if they have children attending school. Probably the worst time of the year to sell property is during the winter, especially at Christmas time. During these holiday times, potential buyers are usually too preoccupied with other things to concern themselves with the purchase of a home. Conversely, since during this time there is a deficiency of buyers, then this time of the year is the best time to make your purchase.

PRICE IT RIGHT

From what you've learned in the appraisal chapter, you should have a realistic idea of what your property is worth. When I say realistic, bear in mind that you're in competition with hundreds of other sellers who are also attempting to sell their properties. And it is very unlikely you'll find a naive buyer willing to pay more for your property than it's actually worth.

To establish the right price, it is first necessary to establish the least you'll accept in price. Then you can adjust your price upwards from this point, allowing a little room for price negotiations. Most buyers like to negotiate, so allow yourself a little flexibility. Therefore, it would then be wise to determine the least you will accept, then price the property reasonably above that point in order to stimulate bona fide offers.

NECESSARY DOCUMENTS AND INFORMATION

After you have decided what price to sell the property for, you can start gathering the documents and information you will need to consummate the sale.

You will need the following information from the loan documents:

- Is there a prepayment penalty on the first mortgage, and, if so, will they waive it if the buyer obtains his mortgage from the same lender?
- What is the current principal balance owing on the loan?
- Is there a tax and insurance impound account, and, if so, what is the balance in that account?

Note that the prepayment penalty is a cost to you, levied by the lender according to the original loan agreement, charging you a penalty (six months' interest is common) for repaying the loan before it's due. This penalty charge covers the lender's cost in reclaiming and then reloaning the money which you paid back prematurely and may be waived, as mentioned earlier.

You will also need the following documents:

- A copy of the paid tax receipt for the previous year
- A copy of the survey of your property
- Evidence of title

HOME-SELLING TIPS

Whether you use the services of a broker, it still will be necessary to prepare the entire property for its eventual sale. The following material is a guide to preparation in order to get a quick and bona fide offer on your property.

Realtors use the phrases "this property has good curb appeal" (i.e., it looks appealing from the curb) or "This house shows well," when showing homes to prospective buyers. Their descriptive jargon is relevant to selling your home, because in order to get the best price for your home it is wise to prepare it to look its best.

Unless you want to sell a fixer-upper, or one that looks like a fixer-upper, one is required to put the house and the surrounding grounds in order so as to get the most out of it. Some of the preparation for the sale can simply be tidying up around the exterior of the house. But, unless you're an extremely tidy housekeeper, which most of us are not, you'll have to do some minor repair and touch-ups to meet good-condition standards. Remember, anything in obvious disrepair will eventually be discounted from the offer price.

First impressions are most favorable. If the house doesn't look appealing from the curb, the prospective buyer might not consider getting out of the car to look further. The following are suggestions that will eventually assist in the quick sale of your home and will get the prospect out of the car and into your home for a further inspection.

Exterior

- Tidy up all around the exterior grounds by removing any debris, old cars, and so on. Cut the grass and trim the hedges and shrubs. Arrange and organize items neatly, such as outdoor furniture and firewood.
- Store away, or have removed from the property, such items as broken-down dishwashers, water heaters, or water softeners. (Avoid the look of a junk yard.)

- Give the lawn a thorough raking and sweep up the sidewalk and driveway.

- Tour the perimeter of your property and repair any broken fencing and paint or stain areas that need attention.

- Carefully inspect your front door. It's one of the first items your home-hunting prospects will examine. If it shows signs of wear, give it a fresh coat of paint or stain. While you're at it, spruce up the house numbers either with a touch-up paint job or replace with new shiny brass ones.

- Quite often repainting the entire exterior of the house isn't necessary. Frequently you can substantially improve the appearance of the house simply by repainting the trim.

- Repair any broken windows or screens, then wash them for a brighter appearance.

Interior

- When you're finished with the exterior, start on the interior of your home. The objective here is to make your home look organized and spacious, bright, warm, and comfortable. I can't emphasize cleanliness enough. Now would be a good time for a thorough spring cleaning. Remember, a clean house will sell much faster than a dirty one.

- Brighten dull rooms with a fresh coat of white, beige, or antique white paint. As I said before, lighter colors make rooms appear bigger and brighter, and neutral colors will go better with the new buyer's furnishings. Instead of taking the time and effort of pulling down old wallpaper and putting up new, try sprucing up the trim instead.

- Cluttered rooms with too much furniture show very poorly. Prospective buyers require lots of room and that's what they're looking for. So rearrange your furniture to make rooms appear more spacious. Put excessive furniture out in storage. De-clutter your home, then rearrange and organize what's left. You'll be surprised how much unwanted stuff can accumulate over the years.

- Now have a giant garage sale to clear out all your unwanted stuff. You can earn extra money to spend on whatever, and you won't have to pay the movers to relocate all those unwanted items.

- Clean all windows and mirrors.

- If the carpet is dirty, have it professionally cleaned. If the carpet appears overly worn, consider having it replaced. It is unlikely you will recover the cost of a new carpet in the sale of your home, but it will likely sell faster.

- Unclutter those kitchen counters to make your kitchen appear more organized and spacious.

- Clean and polish all appliances in the kitchen. Finish in the kitchen by making the sink shiny and sparkling.

- Clean and shine the tub, toilet, and sink in all the bathrooms.

- Now, break out the tool box and start fixing all those little things you've been putting up with all these months. You know, the leaky faucet, loose door knobs, cracked electrical outlets and switch covers. Secure those loose moldings and towel racks and anything that wobbles.

These are all little items of disrepair which can detract from the beauty and function of your home. When a prospective buyer begins examining your home during a walk-through, he is mentally keeping track of any shortcomings. Too many little things in disrepair will bring a lower offer—if any at all—than if the house were in excellent condition.

When it's finally time to show your home to prospective buyers, all the preparations you made will definitely be worth the effort, as your home will receive more and better offers than if you were ill-prepared for the sale. But there are a few additional items you should do just before you show the home that will add that little extra touch of comfort and hominess.

Just before your prospective buyers arrive, clear out the kids and secure the pets where they won't cause any distraction. Turn off the television and put on some soft music. Turn on all the lights in the house to make it as bright as possible, even during the daytime. If you have a fireplace, fire it up also. Liven up the aroma in your home with freshly baked cinnamon rolls right out of the oven. Finish up with clean towels on the racks and put out some fresh flowers to treat yourself for making your home such a tidy showplace.

When the prospects arrive, make yourself scarce (only when using a broker, that is). Your absence will make potential buyers more at ease. Your presence will only distract from the job at hand, that of looking over your entire home and answering any questions, which is the agent's responsibility. If you must be there, try to avoid any conversation with the prospects because the agent needs their full attention to stimulate interest in the features of your home.

Do not complicate the sale of your home by discussing the separate sale of certain appliances, or the fact that you wish to keep certain personal items. Personal property, such as furniture and unattached appliances, can be negotiated later, at a more appropriate time.

Always maintain your home in "showplace condition," as you never know when just the right prospect might show up. Your agent will usually make appointments with you for showings, but if casual browsers drop in for an unexpected visit, it is best not to show your home. Ask for their name and phone number and refer the information to your agent.

Keep in mind that it takes time to sell a home. Be patient. Keep your home on the market for as long as it takes. Your home requires adequate exposure to enough prospective buyers in order to consummate a proper sale.

In closing, you might consider offering a one-year home warranty plan, which would offer a little more added value and overcome questions of the working order of major home systems. These policies are available through most national real estate brokerage companies, and will protect your buyers for one year against most major repairs.

PROPERTY INFORMATION SHEET

The Property Information Sheet is only necessary if you plan to sell the property yourself. It is a list of all the vital measurements and other information about your home, which you will distribute to prospective buyers. Use a 50-foot or longer tape measure to measure each room, and do this as accurately as you can. Enter this and all other stipulated information on the Property Information Sheet that follows, and make copies for distribution.

OPEN HOUSE AND THE "FOR-SALE" SIGN

Traditionally, real estate agents hold open house on their listed properties mostly over weekends. This is the time the majority of potential buyers have the time off from work and can easily go house-hunting.

If you plan to sell your home yourself, weekends would also be the best time to hold your open house. If by chance other owners are holding an open house during the same time as yours, you will actually benefit from it. Numerous open houses in the same neighbor-

PROPERTY INFORMATION SHEET

Address _____ Selling Price $ _____

_____

Existing first mortgage balance _____ at _____%
Existing second mortgage balance _____ at _____%

Monthly payments on first $ _____ plus taxes and insurance $ _____

Monthly payments on second $ _____

Architectural style: _____ Const. _____ Basmt: _____

LR _____	Age: _____	Heat: _____
DR _____	Lot Size: _____	Air cond: _____
Kit _____	Garage: _____	220 Wiring: _____
Dinette: _____	Curbs & gut. _____	Water htr: _____
Fam. rm. _____	Paved st. _____	Water soft: _____
Other rm. _____	Sidewalk: _____	
Bath: _____	Water: _____	
Bath: _____	Sewer: _____	
Bath: _____	Septic: _____	
BR: _____		
BR: _____	Schools: High _____	Grade: _____
BR: _____	Middle _____	
BR: _____		

Draperies and curtains: _____
Carpeting: _____
Items included: Oven _____ Range _____ Frig _____
TV antenna _____ Disposal _____ Dishwasher _____
Items not included: _____

_____

Owner _____ Phone _____

hood means that more prospective buyers will have the opportunity
to see your property.

Unless your property is located on a well-traveled thoroughfare,
you'll need several open house signs to direct prospects to your
property. Count the number of turns a prospect has to make from a
major thoroughfare in order to get to your property. That will be the
number of signs you'll need. Then, get permission from the property
owners where you want to place your signs, and order as many as you
need.

Your open house signs should be 24″ square with red letters on a white background. Each sign will read "OPEN HOUSE" with the appropriate address below, and a red arrow pointing in the correct direction.

The sign in your front yard will read "FOR SALE BY OWNER" in red with your phone number below. In addition to the for-sale sign, consider placing small pennants or flags near the street, which are excellent for arousing attention to your sale.

ADVERTISING

The purpose of your advertising is to get prospects interested enough in your property to come by and look for themselves. Place your ad in the classified section of your Sunday newspaper, because Sundays are when realtors place their ads. Prospective buyers are accustomed to looking for homes in the Sunday paper.

In addition, consider placing an ad for your open house in the Sunday paper. Most newspapers have a separate section classified under "Open House." (For additional information on writing ads, see section in the Property Management chapter on advertising.)

THE SALES AGREEMENT

At this point your property, both inside and out, is tidy and in complete repair. Your advertisements are running and the phone is ringing off the hook with inquiries about your property. Prospective buyers have been walking through your home day after day, and, finally, somebody says they're interested in purchasing your home, or that they wish to sit down and discuss terms of the sale at your earliest convenience. What you have now is not a sale, but a serious and interested prospect. It is now time to negotiate and reduce the details of your negotiations to writing.

Once all the details of price and terms are agreed upon between both you and the buyer, you will complete the Purchase Agreement Checklist, which follows on the next page.

This checklist is used as a guideline in the preparation of documents for completion of sale. Either your escrow agent or an attorney can use this information to avoid having to spend unnecessary time asking questions.

PURCHASE-AGREEMENT CHECKLIST

NOTE: This is not a legally binding agreement. It is simply a checklist to accommodate the drafting of a formal sales agreement between buyer and seller.

Name of prospective buyer(s) _____

_____

currently residing at _____

_____ phone _____

are considering purchasing the property located at _____

_____

for a purchase price of $ _____

Earnest money deposit of $ _____ to be held in escrow

by _____

Buyer to assume existing loans of $ _____

Or, buyer to originate new financing of $ _____

Real estate taxes last year were _____

Contingencies to be included in purchase agreement _____

_____

_____

_____

_____

Items not included in selling price _____

_____

_____

Items that are included in selling price _____

_____

_____

Sellers will vacate the premises on _____

_____

_____

Date of closing escrow _____

Sellers to pay rent of $ _____ per day if sellers occupy premises after the close of escrow.

Legal description of property _____

_____

Qualifying the Buyer

Just because you have a prospect who has announced a readiness to purchase your home, this does not mean that you have a bona fide sale. Many a hopeful buyer will nevertheless lack the adequate income or the credit-worthiness to attain financing, in which case it is futile to enter into a sales agreement with him.

If new financing is to be originated and the buyer has already arranged it, or if he has been told by a lender that he qualifies for a purchase in your price range, then it is not necessary to qualify him beyond getting proof of the above. In all other cases (loan assumption or a wrap-around loan) you must obtain certain information and qualify the buyer yourself. (For additional information on qualifying the buyer, see chapter on financing for qualification procedure.)

SUMMARY

We can now compare the total cost of selling the property yourself with the cost of having the same property sold by a real estate broker who receives a 6 percent commission. Assuming a $80,000 selling price, the broker's commission would be $4,800 ($80,000 × 6 %). When you deduct your own costs of sale from this amount, that will be your savings.

The following are approximate costs you incur in selling the property yourself, not including normal closing costs which have to paid regardless of whether you use a broker or not:

```
"For Sale" signs:  ...........................  $ 60
Advertising  ................................   100
Copies of information sheet  .................     5
Total cost  .................................  $165
```

Thus, you will make $4,635 ($4,800 − $165), or save that much, if you look at it that way, by selling the house yourself.

13 THE 1986 INCOME TAX RULES FOR REAL ESTATE

HIGHLIGHTS OF CHANGES IN TAX REFORM ACT OF 1986

The Tax Reform Act of 1986 features many dramatic changes which will extensively affect market values, rents, income, and rates of return—of most real estate investments. This chapter will attempt to simplify the complicated rules covering real estate and try to assist you at profitable real estate investment.

The significant decrease in tax rate from a maximum of 50 percent under prior law to 28 percent under the new law will definitely alter tax-planning strategies for the future. Depreciation as the tax-shelter benefit of real estate will, under the 1986 law, be worth only 28 cents on the dollar (instead of 50 cents under the old law). Furthermore, with the new passive loss limitations, certain real estate investors will be limited as to how many write-offs can be allocated toward other income.

Tax reform definitely simplified the tax system for many taxpayers, but the new laws have severely complicated tax rules for the real estate investor and homeowner. It is the objective of this chapter to unravel these complexities and assist you in tax planning, enabling you to work proficiently with your tax planner or attorney in making future correct decisions.

Those changes in the new Tax Reform Act of 1986 which will affect real estate are highlighted below:

- There are passive income and loss limitation rules.
- The 60 percent deduction for capital gains has been repealed. After 1986, capital gains are to be taxed as ordinary income.
- New tax rates have been substantially reduced.
- The deduction for nonmortgage-interest (personal) expense has been repealed and will eventually be phased out.

- There is a limit on mortgage-interest deduction, not to exceed the cost of the home being mortgaged.
- Rules on installment sales of real property under certain conditions have been changed.
- Depreciation of real property purchased after 1986 have been dramatically changed.

Before we unravel the latest changes in tax laws, the following is information on how you, the homeowner, can save money on income taxes.

HOMEOWNER TAX SAVINGS

You can avoid or defer tax on the gain from the sale of your home depending on certain conditions and your age.

Item 1: Deferring Tax on the Sale of a Residence
You can defer tax on the gain from the sale of your home if you meet the following three tests:

1. *Principal residence test.* This test requires that you have used your old house as your principal residence and you now use, or intend to use, your new house as a principal residence. Only one principal residence, for tax deferral purposes, is allowed at any one time. You cannot defer tax on the profitable sale of a principal residence by buying a summer cottage, nor can you defer the tax on the sale of a second home.

2. *Time test.* This test requires that within two years of the sale of your old house you buy, or build, and use your new house as a principal residence.

3. *Investment test.* This test requires that you buy or build a house equal to, or more than, the amount you received from the sale of the old house. If the replacement house costs less, part or all of the gain is taxed. Tax deferring is mandatory when you qualify under the above three tests.

Exchanging houses or trading is considered the same as a sale for tax deferral purposes. If you make an even exchange, or pay additional cash, there is no tax on the trade. However, if you receive cash in the trade for the replacement house, you generally realize a taxable gain.

Item 2: Tax-Free Residence Sale if Age 55 or Older

You can avoid tax on profits up to $125,000 once in a lifetime if you are 55 or older when you sell or exchange your principal residence. In order to claim this exclusion, you must: (1) elect to avoid tax; (2) be 55 or older before the date of sale; and (3) for at least three years prior to the sale have owned and occupied the house as your principal residence. You cannot use this exclusion when you sell only a partial interest in the home.

If you and your spouse own the home jointly and file a joint return in the year of the sale, only one of you need meet the age requirement of 55 or older and qualify under ownership and residency requirements three out of the last five years.

Use caution when taking the tax-free election. Because this is a once-in-a-lifetime exclusion, consider using the tax deferral method under Item 1 when the gain from the sale of your home is substantially less than the $125,000 exclusion and you plan to reinvest the proceeds in a replacement home. If, for example, you did qualify for the $125,000 exclusion, and after the sale of your home the gain was only $15,000 and you elected to exclude it, you will have used up your once-in-a-lifetime exclusion. You could defer this gain if you buy a replacement house at a cost equal to or more than the sales price of the old house. Then, later when you sell the replacement house without a further home purchase, the election to exclude the gain can then be made.

Refinancing

Generally speaking, the points you pay to refinance your principal residence are not deductible, regardless of how you pay them, if they are not paid in connection with the purchase or improvement of the home. However, the portion of points is deductible if you use a part of the proceeds to make an improvement on your principal residence and you pay the costs out of your private funds (rather than out of the proceeds of the new loan). The amount apportioned for the improvement can either be deducted in full in the year you pay it, or you may also deduct the apportioned amount over the life of the loan.

Deducting Expenses When Renting Out Part of Your Home

That part of your home you occupy is handled differently for tax purposes from the rented part. Rental income and expenses allocated to the rented part of the property are reported on Schedule E. The expenses allocated to the rental part are deductible, whether or not you itemize deductions. Deductions for interest and taxes on your personal part of the property are itemized deductions. For example, you bought a fourplex in 1972 and you occupy one unit as a personal residence. You purchased it for $50,000 ($42,000 for the building and $8,000 for the land). You determined that it has a useful life of 30 years. The following is how you deduct expenses:

Depreciation: 75% of bldg. (purchase price, $42,000)	Cost basis: $31,500	Useful life: 30 years	Depreciation: $1,050

	Total	Deduct itemized deductions	Deduct on rent schedule	Not deductible
Interest	$1,600	$400	$1,200	
Taxes	800	200	600	
Repairs	100		75	$25
Depreciation	1,050		1,050	
	$3,550	$600	$2,925	$25

Repair expense apportioned to your personal unit are nondeductible personal expenses. Other expenses apportioned to personal use are deductible, provided your itemized deductions are in excess of your zero-bracket amount.

Depreciation after conversion of home to rental. If you convert your residence to a rental property, you can begin to take the depreciation on the building. The amount of depreciation allowed is based on whichever is lower, the building's fair market value at the time of conversion or the adjusted cost basis (original purchase price plus capital improvements until time of conversion).

Basis to use on a sale of rental. If you sell and realize a profit, then you use the adjusted cost basis at the time of conversion less depreciation. If you sell and realize a loss, you use the lower of adjusted cost basis or fair market value at the time of conversion, less depreciation.

NEW RULES FOR VACATION HOMES

The new tax law prohibits most homeowners from deducting losses (expenses in excess of income) while renting out a personal vacation

Review of Changes

Old Law	1986 Reforms
Mortgage interest is fully deductible	Mortgage interest is deductible only on first and second homes
Deductible losses are not limited on vacation homes	Deductible losses on rented vacation homes limited to $25,000; this cap is reduced when adjusted gross income is over $100,000

home. A vacation home can be a condominium, apartment, house trailer, motor home, boat, or house. Certain tests are formulated to disallow losses. These tests are based on the days of rental and personal usage. The following tests will determine whether you are allowed losses: (1) If the vacation home is rented for less than 15 days, you cannot deduct expenses allocated to the rental (except for interest and real estate taxes). If you sell and realize a profit on the rental, the profit is not taxable.

(2) If the vacation home is rented for 15 days or more, then you have to determine if your personal use of the home exceeds a 14-day or 10 percent time test (10% of the number of days the home is rented). If it does, then you are considered to have used the home as a residence during the year and rental expenses are deductible only to the extent of gross rental income. Therefore, if gross rental income exceeds expenses, the operating gain is fully taxable.

(3) If you rent the vacation home for 15 days or more, but your rental usage is less than the 14-day/10-percent test, then you are not considered to have made personal use of the residence during the year. In this case, expenses in excess of gross rental income may be deductible. Previous tax court cases have allowed loss deductions when the owner made little personal use of the vacation home and proved to have bought the house to earn a profitable amount in resale.

INTEREST DEDUCTIONS

Deducting Interest Paid on a Home Mortgage

Tax reform has placed certain limitations on the ability to deduct interest as an expense on a home mortgage. Under the new rules you are now allowed to deduct home mortgage interest only up to the original purchase price of the home and the cost of home improve-

Review of Changes

Old Law	1986 Reforms
All home mortgage interest is fully deductible	Mortgage interest is deductible on two homes only.
All personal interest is fully deductible	The personal-interest deduction is to be phased out between 1987 and 1991
Interest deductions on investments are limited to net investment income plus $10,000	Interest deductions on investments are limited to the amount of net-investment income

ments. Additional amounts, but not more than the fair market value of the home, can be borrowed for educational and medical expenses with the interest still remaining deductible. To qualify the home has to be used as security for the debt.

For example, you purchased a home for $80,000, and three years later you added on a den costing $12,000. You are limited in the amount of financing on which interest can be deducted to $92,000. If you borrowed $100,000, the interest on the additional $8,000 loan would not be deductible as home-mortgage interest. Since the additional loan of $8,000 is above the $92,000 limit, it will be treated as personal-consumer interest which is only deductible to the extent allowed by the new consumer-interest phaseout rules. On the other hand, if the additional $8,000 was used for medical or educational costs, the interest would then be deductible.

What home improvements qualify to increase the amount you can borrow? A home improvement is considered generally to include all expenditures that will add value to your home and last for an extended period, such as, swimming pool, new roof, new patio or deck, siding, built-in appliances, built-in cabinets, alarm system, hot water heater, new sidewalk, replacement windows, insulation, and certain landscaping.

What mortgage loans are affected by these new rules? All home loans originated after August 16, 1986, are subject to the new rules. Home mortgage loans that were outstanding on this date will not be affected unless they exceed the fair market value of the home at that date. Also, the mortgage interest on one additional home, such as a vacation home, will qualify for the mortgage interest deduction. To qualify for a second vacation home, see new rules for vacation homes above.

NEW RULES FOR THE HOME OFFICE

Review of Changes

Old Law	1986 Reforms
Employee can claim a home-office deduction when employer rents a portion of his house as an office	Rental arrangements between employers and employees are disallowed
Home-office deduction cannot exceed taxpayer's gross income from trade or business	Home-office deduction is limited to net income from trade or business
	Home-office deduction in excess of net income can be carried forward to future years

New Rules for Business Use of Your Home

In order to claim a deduction for a home office the office must be used exclusively for an office (the room where your wife watches television or sews while you work does not qualify) and on a regular basis. The office in the home must be used for: (1) actually meeting patients or customers (making phone calls to patients or customers won't qualify); or (2) as the primary place of business. Taxpayers can operate more than one business for the purpose of this test; therefore employees can moonlight in another business and claim a home office deduction as long as they qualify under the other tests. In addition, an employee can claim home office deductions if the office is maintained for the convenience of the employer. An unattached structure to the home used in connection with the taxpayer's business will also qualify.

According to the 1986 Act, certain deductions are allowed for a home office, such as depreciation, insurance, utilities, and so on, which can offset income realized from that business. These deductions can only be claimed up to the net income of that business.

For example, an employee operates a separate business out of his home as a writer. He earned $4,400 in royalties during the year. His expenses for the year were: postage and office supplies $920; subscriptions $1,280; depreciation on his home office $2,400; utilities $200; and insurance on his home office $90. Deductions for depreciation, insurance, and utilities can only be used to the extent of the net income of the home business determined without these items. See the following:

Royalties		$4,400
Expenses other than home office		
Postage and office supplies	$ 920	
Subscriptions	1,280	
Subtotal	2,200	2,200
Net income before		
home office deductions		$2,200

In the above example, this taxpayer's deductions for home office are limited to $2,200. Home-office expenses cannot be used as a tax loss to offset other income. Although he has a total of $2,690 in home-office expenses (depreciation $2,400 + $200   utilities + $90 insurance = $2,690), he is left with $490 in unused deductions that can be carried forward and used against business income in future years.

Home-office expenses are considered a miscellaneous itemized deduction, which means they are subject to the same limitations imposed on all miscellaneous itemized deductions: a deduction can only be allowed when that total miscellaneous deduction exceeds 2 percent of the taxpayer's income.

1986 RULES FOR DEPRECIATION

Depreciation is the percentage reduction in loss of value of an asset over its physical life. It is strictly a bookkeeping entry, which is not an out-of-pocket expense to the investor. The Tax Reform Act of 1986 has dramatically reduced the benefits of depreciation in a number of ways. The number of years an asset can be written off has been lengthened from 19 years to 27.5 years, and 31.5 years in certain cases. Also, accelerated methods have been eliminated, thus reducing benefits during the early years of the holding period. And, because of the new lower tax rates, depreciation tax benefits are not worth as much as they were before tax reform.

Generally speaking, if you buy property to use in a trade or business, or to earn rent or royalty income, and the property has a useful life of more than one year, you cannot deduct its entire cost in one year. Instead, you must spread the cost over more than one year and deduct a part of it each year. For most types of property, this is called depreciation.

Review of Changes

Old Law	1986 Reforms
Income property is depreciated over 19 years	Residential rentals are depreciated over 27.5 years; commercial rentals at 31.5 years
Income property is depreciated either by straight-line or accelerated methods	Only straight-line method of depreciation is allowed on income property
Real estate investments are not subject to "at-risk" rules	Real estate investments are subject to "at-risk" rules
Vehicles are depreciated over 3 years	Vehicles are depreciated over 5 years
Most machinery and equipment is depreciated over 5 years	Most machinery and equipment is depreciated over 7 years
Personal property is depreciated using the 150 percent declining balance method	Personal property is depreciated using the 200 percent declining balance method

What Can Be Depreciated?
Many different kinds of property can be depreciated, such as machinery, buildings, vehicles, patents, copyrights, furniture, and equipment. Property is depreciable if it meets all three of these tests:

1. It must be used in business or held for the production of income (e.g., to earn rent or royalty income).
2. It must have a useful life that can be determined, and its useful life must be longer than one year. The useful life of a piece of property is an estimate of how long you can expect to use it in your business or to earn rent or royalty income.
3. It must be something that wears out, decays, gets used up, becomes obsolete, or loses value from natural causes.

Depreciable property may be tangible (i.e., it can be seen or touched) or intangible. Intangible property includes such items as a copyright or franchise. Depreciable property may be personal or real. Personal property is property, such as machinery and equipment that is not real estate. Real property is land and generally anything that is erected on, growing on, or attached to land. However, the land itself is not depreciable.

Depreciation not only serves the purpose of determining taxable income, but it is also the essence of why real estate has been a "tax shelter." Historically real estate investors have been able to earn substantial net income free of taxes from their properties, and in certain cases while actually showing taxable losses that could be written off against salary income. Thus the tax-shelter benefit of real estate, because the taxable loss (which in reality is actually a net gain, or profit) can shelter salary income from other sources.

Figuring Depreciation—Old Rules and 1986 Rules

Since the benefits of depreciation have been greatly reduced under the 1986 Tax Reform Act, it is important to understand the two basic types of assets, each of which is depreciable using different rules. One can obtain valuable tax savings by carefully drawing distinctions between these two types of property.

Depreciating Buildings—Old Rules. Before the Tax Reform Act of 1986, most real property was depreciated over a 19-year period. These write-offs were figured either using the straight-line method (an equal amount of depreciation annually over its physical life), or by using a more accelerated method (almost double the straight-line method during the early years of its physical life). Even though the accelerated method offered more deductions in earlier years, the straight-line method was often selected in order to avoid rules requiring the taxpayer to "recapture" (give back) certain depreciation upon the sale of the property.

In addition, prior rules required you to use one half-month's depreciation deduction in the month you purchased, or put the building in use. This rule is referred to as the "mid-month convention."

Depreciating Equipment and Fixtures—Old Rules. Under prior rules most personal property was written off over five years, usually at an accelerated method of depreciation. Also, only one half-year of depreciation deduction was allowed in the year the asset was purchased or built (referred to as the "half-year convention").

Depreciating Buildings—1986 Rules. Now under the Tax Reform Act, real property must be written off over much longer periods, with the accelerated methods available under previous rules no longer being available. Therefore, only the straight-line method can be used. However, the mid-month convention still can be used. In addition, the Reform Act rules extended the application of the mid-month convention to include all real property, as opposed to the old rules which limited certain property.

Under the 1986 law, residential and nonresidential property have different depreciation periods. Residential real estate is depreciated over a 27.5-year period, and nonresidential real estate (commercial real estate such as office buildings and shopping centers) is depreciated over a 31.5-year period. Residential property is defined as a building with 80 percent or more of its rental income derived from dwelling units. A dwelling unit is defined as an apartment or house used to provide living accommodations. This does not include hotels or motels which rent more than half of their capacity on a temporary basis. And if you reside in one of the apartments, then a fair rental value can be allocated to your living unit.

Comparing Depreciation Benefits—Old Rules versus 1986 Rules. How much has the 1986 tax law reduced the value of your depreciation benefits? To find out let's compare the results the investor got with what he would have received under the old law. For the purpose of simplicity, assume that under both rulings the straight-line method is used and that all tax benefits are received at year end.

The difference in tax benefits annually is $3,227, which is substantial. Notice that the new tax rule of extending the term of the write-off from 19 years to 27.5 years is only part of the cause in the differential. The substantial reduction in tax rate is also responsible for the reduced benefit.

OLD RULES

Depreciation ($200,000 cost for 19 years)	$10,526
Tax rate	× 50%
Annual tax benefit	$ 5,263

1986 RULES

Depreciation ($200,000 cost for 27.5 years)	$ 7,273
Tax rate	× 28%
Annual tax benefit	$ 2,036

Depreciating Certain Land Improvements. Under the 1986 rules, certain land improvements are depreciated over 15 years using the 150 percent declining-balance method. Conversion to the straight-line method at the time that maximizes deductions is also allowed. Depreciable land improvements are items such as bridges, roads, sidewalks, and landscaping. Sewer pipes are depreciated over a 20-year period. Buildings and their improvements are not allowed under this method.

Depreciating Equipment and Fixtures—1986 Rules. Personal property, such as vehicles, equipment, or furniture, is generally written off by using the accelerated 200 percent declining-balance method over a five- or seven-year period. For example, most cars and light trucks will be depreciated over five years. Most office furniture, fixtures, and equipment (desks, safes, and certain communication equipment) will be depreciated over seven years. The half-year convention also applies to personal property. (Note that the accelerated methods of 150 percent and 200 percent declining balance are calculated at one-and-a-half, and twice, respectively, the rate of the straight-line method.) The following example of the declining-balance method illustrates how this method works for five-year property.

The 1986 rules permit a switch to the straight-line method when it will provide a larger deduction. In the fifth year the 200 percent declining balance method would provide a deduction of $830 (40% × $2,074). Switching to the straight-line method in the fifth year provides a deduction of $1,382 ($2,074 of costs not yet written off, divided by the 1.5 years remaining in the depreciation period). The half-year convention causes the depreciation period to be extended to a sixth year.

The calculations for seven-year property and the 150 percent declining-balance method of depreciation are similar, except that under the 150 percent method one-and-a-half times the straight-line method is used (30 % instead of 40 %) in the depreciation-rate column.

Example of the 200 percent Declining-Balance Method

Year	(Declining Balance) Cost—Depreciation	Depreciation Rate	Amount of Depreciation
1	$12,000	40% × .5 (half)	$2,400
2	9,600	40%	3,840
3	5,760	40%	2,304
4	3,456	40%	1,382
5	2,074	—	1,382
6	692	—	692
			$12,000

"At-Risk" Rules—Changes Since 1986

Under the old law, real estate was exempt from the government's strict "at-risk" rules. The 1986 rules treat real estate the same as other investment activities.

At-risk rules limit the amount of losses you can deduct. Specifically, these losses (deductions) cannot exceed the total of:

- the cash you contribute to the business;
- the adjusted basis of your property contributions to the business; and
- the amount you borrowed for the business, but only to the extent you pledge other assets or have personal liability as security for the borrowing. The exception to this is financing secured only by the property itself, called "qualified nonrecourse financing." To qualify, the nonrecourse financing must be:
  - secured only by the real property;
  - actual debt (not disguised equity similar to convertible debt); and
  - obtained from a qualified lender, such as an institutional lender or related party. (If obtained from a related party, such as the seller or the promoter of the investment, the loan is required to be at reasonable market rates similar to those made to unrelated parties.)

1986 RULES FOR PASSIVE LOSSES

A "passive activity" is any activity that involves the conduct of any trade or business in which you do not materially participate. *Any rental activity will be a passive activity even if you materially participate in it.* A trade or business includes any activity involving research or experimentation and, to the extent provided in the regulations, any activity in connection with a trade or business, or any activity for which a deduction is allowed as an expense for the production of income. You are considered to materially participate if you are involved in the operation of the activity on a regular, continuous, and substantial basis. Participation by your spouse will be considered in determining if you materially participate.

For the tax years beginning after 1986, your deductions from passive activities may only be used to offset your income from passive activities. Any excess deductions result in a "passive-activity loss"

Review of Changes

Old Law	1986 Law
No limitations on deductions of losses on real estate	Deductible losses on real estate are limited to $25,000, reduced for adjusted gross over $100,000
Losses are deductible regardless of whether you actively participate in managing the property	Losses are not deductible inside the $25,000 cap unless you actively participate in managing the property
Losses from real estate can be used to offset other income sources	Losses in excess of $25,000 can be used only to offset gains from other passive investments

and may not be deducted against your other income but may be carried over and applied against passive income in future years. In addition, any allowable credits from passive activity may only be used to offset your tax liability allocable to your passive activities. Any excess "passive-activity credit" may not be claimed against your tax liability on your other income but may be carried over and applied against tax on passive activity income in future years.

These rules apply to any individual, estate, trust, closely held C corporation, or personal service corporation. They do not apply to any carryovers from a tax year beginning before 1987. Fiscal year (1986–87) entities, such as partnerships and S corporations, must separately report their passive activity items to their partners and shareholders so that they may properly reflect them on their 1987 tax return.

Example
Three Types of Income for Passive-Loss Rules

Active	Passive	Portfolio
Employee wages	Most rental real estate	Interest
Primary trade or business	Net leased realty	Dividends
Real estate development	Limited partnership	REIT (Real Estate Investment Trust) distributions
Active retailer	No material participation	Royalties
Consultant		

Now to illustrate the impact of the new passive-loss limitations. For example, assume an investor with an aversion to paying income taxes has purchased real estate tax shelters in the past from a syndicator for the purpose of sheltering his other income. His other sources of income are salary from his job as an executive of a corporation, dividends and interest, and investments in several tax shelters.

Salary	$ 150,000
Dividends	21,000
Interest	14,000
Tax-shelter losses	(183,000)
Taxable income before exemptions	$ 2,000

After taking into consideration his personal exemption, the investor in this example would in fact owe no tax. His income under the new rules will fall into three categories as follows: Salary of $150,000 under the active income category, dividends and interest under the portfolio category, and tax shelter losses under the passive income category.

Now under the 1986 rules he will generally not be allowed to use the losses from the passive-income category to offset income and gains from the other categories. Therefore, once these new provisions are effective, he will no longer be able to avoid paying taxes. He will have an income of $185,000 ($150,000 active income and $35,000 portfolio income). In the year 1988 he will owe a tax of $51,800 ($185,000 × 28 %), overlooking standard deductions. This dramatic result is exactly what Congress sought to achieve when it made changes to investment taxation under the Tax Reform Act of 1986.

Certain Passive-Income Losses Can Offset Other Income

As mentioned before, an interest in real estate rental activity, no matter how much you participate, will not be considered an active business. This means that losses from real estate investments are only allowed to offset income and gains from other passive investments. Therefore, real estate losses cannot shelter wage or active business income. However, there is a major exception to this rule to assist moderate-income taxpayers who invest in real estate.

Certain investors can apply passive-income losses to wage earnings or income from an active business. In order to qualify for this real estate loss exception (up to a maximum of $25,000) the investor must meet both an income and participation test. The investor's adjusted gross income must be less than $150,000. The entire $25,000 loss allowance is permitted for taxpayers with adjusted gross income up to $100,000. The $25,000 loss allowance is reduced by 50 percent of the amount by which the adjusted gross income is more than $100,000. Thus, if the adjusted gross income exceeds $150,000, this allowance rule will not apply.

The other requirement to qualify for this loss allowance is that the investor must "actively participate." (This rule is not as stringent as other participation tests, as you will soon see.) To get the benefit of up to $25,000 in tax losses, the investor is required to meet the following two tests:

1. The investor must own at least 10 percent of the value of the activity during the entire year which he is the owner.

2. The investor is required to make management decisions or arrange for others to provide such services. It is not necessary for the investor to do certain things directly, such as repairs or approving prospective tenants. The hiring of a repair man and a rental agent does not violate the participation test; however caution should be taken if you hire a management company to operate the property. The property-management agreement should clearly indicate that the investor is involved in the decision-making process.

Passive-Income Losses are Carried Forward

Those losses the investor couldn't use during one tax year are not lost forever. In fact, they are carried forward as "suspended losses" and used in one of two ways:

1. If the investor has unused losses incurred in prior years and carried forward, he can apply those losses against income or gains in the passive-income category in future years. Under the old rules the losses would have been used to shelter income from other sources. However, under the new rules they will be used to shelter the income in later years for the same or other passive-income investments.

2. Unused suspended losses from prior years can be used to reduce any gain you realize when you dispose of your investment.

In determining income or loss from an activity, do not consider any (a) gross income from interest, dividends, annuities, or royalties not derived in the ordinary course of a trade or business; (b) expenses (other than interest) that are clearly and directly allocable to such income; (c) interest expense properly allocable to such income; and (d) gain or loss from the disposition of property producing such income or held for investment. Any interest in a passive activity is not treated as property held for investment. In addition, you do not include wages, salaries, professional fees, or other amounts received as compensation for services rendered as income from a passive activity.

Rental Real Estate Activity

An individual will be allowed a deduction for any passive-activity loss or the deduction equivalent of the passive-activity credit for any tax year from rental real estate activities in which he actively participated. The amount allowed under this rule, however, cannot be more than $25,000 (or $12,500 for a married individual filing separately). This amount is reduced by 50 percent of the amount by which your adjusted gross income is more than $100,000 ($50,000 for married filing separately). Therefore, if your adjusted gross income exceeds $150,000 ($75,000 for married filing separately), this allowance rule will not apply.

EFFECTIVE DATES OF THE NEW PASSIVE-LOSS RULES

Finally, you have to take into consideration when these new rules go into effect. Beginning in 1987, these new rules are effective for all losses. However, for investments made prior to October 22, 1986, when the Tax Reform Act was enacted, these new rules are phased in over a five-year period. The following percentages of your losses are disallowed each year:

Year	Loss Disallowed
1987	35%
1988	60
1989	80
1990	90
1991 and after	100%

NOTE: Special care should be taken regarding the alternative minimum tax (AMT) because there is no phase-in of the passive-loss rules for the AMT. You may not get any immediate benefit from your passive losses if you're subject to the AMT. Furthermore, if you have incurred passive losses before tax reform, and passive gains after tax reform, the profits on these latter investments have to be netted against your passive losses before these phase-in rules can be used.

ALTERNATIVE MINIMUM TAX (AMT)

Owing to the complexities of the new AMT, only a brief overview of what it is deserves mention here. The entire subject of the AMT requires an accountant's attention to enable you to get a thorough understanding of the subject and to learn whether you qualify under the rules of the AMT. Generally, only the wealthiest and the most heavily sheltered taxpayers have to concern themselves with the AMT.

Under the old law, taxpayers were subject to a 20 percent minimum tax. Under the 1986 law, taxpayers are subject to a 21 percent minimum tax, and computational changes and new concepts are introduced that further complicate what is complicated already.

Before the Tax Reform Act of 1986, Congress for many years found it appropriate to encourage long-term investment in production facilities so as to improve America's competitive edge. One of the incentives used to promote this type of investment was the preferential treatment of capital gains, which allowed taxpayers to exclude 60 percent of any gain realized from the sale of an asset. This incentive to promote capital formation was a worthy goal of the Congress, but so was tax equity. Therefore, in order to maintain a certain amount of fairness in the tax system, Congress decided that everyone should pay at least a minimum amount of tax which resulted in the Alternative Minimum Tax. (For more information on the Alternative Minimum Tax for individuals, including the new rules, see Publication 909, Alternative Minimum Tax.)

LONG-TERM CAPITAL GAINS: LAST CHANCE TO CASH IN

The preferential treatment of capital gains has traditionally been one of the most important benefits for real estate investors. Before tax reform, capital gains rules allowed the taxpayer to exclude 60 percent of the gain realized on the sale of an asset for tax purposes. Now under the new rules, capital gains benefits have been repealed, and all gains realized in the sale of an asset have to be taxed as regular income.

In addition, Congress changed the taxation on installment sales. An installment sale is one in which the seller takes back a mortgage and the buyer pays for the property over an extended term. Under the previous rules, the seller would report a portion of each payment

REVIEW OF CHANGES

Old Law	1986 Reforms
Sixty percent of long-term capital gains can be excluded from taxable income	You can no longer exclude 60 percent of long-term capital gains
The results of the 60 percent exclusion were a top capital gain tax rate of 20 percent	Capital gains are taxed as ordinary income, except in 1987, when the capital gain rate is capped at 28 percent

received as profit subject to tax. New tax reform legislation has made a number of changes to this rule.

New Capital Gains Rules

As mentioned before, the 60 percent exclusion afforded capital gains has been repealed under the new rules. The new law incorporates a phase-in (transition period), setting five tax rates during the tax year 1987. All capital gains after 1987 will be taxed just like ordinary income once the new law is completely effective. Under the reform law the following schedule illustrates the new tax rates:

New Tax Rates

Taxable Income Brackets

Tax Rate	Married filing joint return	Married filing separate return	Heads of household	Single individuals
11%	0-$3,000	0-$1,500	0-$2,500	0-$1,800
15	$3,001-28,000	$1,501-14,000	$2,501-23,000	$1,801-16,800
28	28,001-45,000	14,001-22,500	23,001-38,000	16,801-27,000
35	45,001-90,000	22,501-45,000	38,001-80,000	27,000-54,000
38.5	over 90,000	over 45,000	over 80,000	over 54,000

1988 and after
Taxable Income Brackets

Tax Rate	Married filing joint return	Married filing separate return	Heads of household	Single individuals
15%	0-$29,750	0-$14,875	0-$23,900	0-$17,850
28	over 29,750	over 14,875	over 23,900	over 17,850

According to the new rules, an individual taxpayer's income will be grouped together and subject to the applicable tax rates on the preceding schedule. However, under a special rule, capital gains will be limited to a maximum rate of 28 percent during the transition year of 1987. Therefore, for the 1987 tax year your ordinary income will be taxed up to the rate of 38.5 percent, excluding capital gains, which will be taxed at a maximum rate of 28 percent.

New Rules on Installment Sales

To understand the new rules since tax reform which affect installment sales it will be necessary to review prior rules (most of which are still applicable) that existed before tax reform. The intent of Congress in changing the tax laws was simplification; however the actual result was to make the new rules more complex, especially in the area of the installment sale.

If you sold a real estate investment and realized the entire sales price in the year of the sale, the entire gain would be taxable in the year the sale took place. An alternative to this would be for the seller to accept a down payment and take back a purchase-money mortgage for the balance owing wherein the buyer would pay principal and interest on the unpaid balance over an extended period of time. This would be considered an installment sale.

How much of the deferred payments under an installment sale are taxable? The rules state that to determine the taxable amount of income of each payment the gross profit ratio is applied to each payment received. The gross profit ratio is computed by dividing the taxable gain (gross profit) by the total sales price.

For example, you sell your residence for $200,000 which you paid $50,000 for 10 years ago. Therefore, you have a taxable gain of $150,000 ($200,000 sales price less your $50,000 investment). The sales price of $200,000 is the amount you will receive. What portion of each deferred payment do you report as income?

$$\text{Gross Profit Ratio} = \frac{\text{Taxable Gain of \$150,000}}{\text{Total Sales Price of \$200,000}} = 75\%$$

Therefore, from the above example, 75 percent of the down payment and each additional deferred payment will be reported as income.

In the event the buyer, from the above example, were to assume an existing mortgage, the total sales price for the purpose of this calculation would be reduced by the amount of such mortgage. For example, the buyer assumes an existing mortgage of $25,000 in addition to making deferred payments on a purchase-money mortgage to you. Therefore, the total sales price would be reduced by $25,000 and different gross profit calculations have to be made.

Total Sales Price	$200,000
Mortgage Assumed	25,000
New Sales Price	$175,000

Now under these circumstances the portion of each payment that is considered income is 85.71 percent ($150,000 taxable gain divided by the new sales price of $175,000).

Borrowing Against Your Installment Notes. Up to this point, all the existing tax rules regarding installment sales are applicable to today's tax laws. New rules apply to the disposition of funds acquired when an investor borrows against (uses as collateral) such installment notes. Prior to tax reform many taxpayers could obtain cash without triggering the unreported gain by pledging their installment notes as collateral for loans. For example, from the above illustration, you could have used the $150,000 notes as collateral for a loan up to this amount from an unrelated financial institution. Since the borrowing of funds would not have been treated as a sale of the notes, you could have obtained cash without triggering a gain on the installment notes.

The new tax reform rules attempt to deny the availability of the installment sale method to the extent of total borrowings through the new "proportionate disallowance rule." This rule tries to determine what portion of your total borrowings relate to the installment notes you're holding. Congress felt it appropriate since an installment sale received fair treatment by only taxing that part of the gain received each year. However, if you borrow against these deferred payments and now have all the cash, the tax deferred under the installment sale should be paid.

Because it is often difficult to determine which assets were pledged to support which liabilities, average figures are used to compute a ratio. In order to determine this average ratio, you divide applicable installment debt by your total assets and multiply the result by your average borrowings. The resulting percentage will provide a rough estimate of how much of your borrowings are attributable to the installment notes you hold. See illustration below.

$$\frac{\text{Installment Notes}}{\text{Total Assets}} \times \text{Average Borrowings} = \frac{\text{Deemed Payment on}}{\text{Installment Obligations}}$$

Special Rules and Exceptions to the Installment Sale. First of all, the above-mentioned rules do not apply to the installment sale of your personal residence. Most farm property is also excluded.

The disposal of certain timeshare property and unimproved land is not subject to the proportionate disallowance rule if the buyer's obligation to repay the installment notes is not guaranteed or insured by a third party. In addition, neither the seller or any of his affiliates may develop the land. Due to this special treatment the seller is required to pay interest on the deferred tax liability.

Sale of public traded property, such as REITs, cannot be reported under the installment method.

Sales of property subject to the passive-loss limitation rules sold under the installment-sale method require certain attention. The suspended passive losses (the unused portion), will be recognized in each year in the ratio of the profit realized in that year to the total profit to be realized on the transaction. In order to trigger realization of the entire loss in the year of the sale you must elect not to have the installment sales rules apply.

In conclusion, a major change in the prohibition of the use of the installment sale method altogether for purposes of the alternative minimum tax. This rule applies to anyone subject to the proportionate disallowance rule. This will include investors involved with residential subdividing, the sale of real estate used in trade or business, and rental real estate where the purchase price exceeds $150,000.

Under these circumstances, especially if you're subject to the alternative minimum tax, an installment sale will not benefit you. It is therefore recommended that you structure your real estate sales so that you realize enough cash in the year of the sale to pay any tax due.

TAX CREDITS FOR LOW-INCOME HOUSING AND REHABILITATION

New Tax Credit for Low-Income Rental Housing

Tax reform has created new incentives based on a two-tier tax credit for encouraging the construction or rehabilitation of low-income rental housing. The two-tier credit system offers a different tax credit for different types of qualifying expenditures. A 9 percent tax credit is available for new construction and rehabilitation expenditures placed in service in 1987. A 4 percent tax credit is available for the cost of acquiring an existing building in 1987, or new or existing construction which is financed with federal subsidies. Each tax credit is avail-

REVIEW OF CHANGES

Old Law	1986 Reforms
No tax credit is available for low-income housing	Low-income housing credit is 9% of construction cost, or 4% of the acquisition cost
Rehabilitation credit is 15% for 30-year old buildings, 20% for those older than 40, and 25% for certified historic structures (CHS)	Credit is reduced to 10% for non-CHS structures built before 1936; 20% for CHS
Investment tax credit (ITC) is from 4 to 10% of qualifying property	(ITC) is repealed

able every year for 10 years. After 1987, the structure of the tax credits will remain generally the same. However, each tax credit rate will be revised by the IRS on a monthly basis in order to reflect changes in market interest rates.

As an example of the tax-credit savings available, consider the following: over 10 years on a $100,000 qualifying expenditure you could generate $9,000 (or $4,000) in credit annually for 10 years, or a sum of $90,000.

How to Qualify

Certain requirements must be met to qualify for the low-income housing credit.

1. A minimum portion of the building must be reserved for use by low-income families. This can be achieved in one of two ways, and the owner must irrevocably select which one of the two ways that will be used. The first test to qualify requires that 20 percent or more of the entire project be occupied by families or individuals having incomes no greater than one-half that of the median-income level for that area. The second test requires that 40 percent or more of the entire project be occupied by families or individuals with incomes no more than 60 percent of the median income for that area.

2. The available units must both be suitable and be used for occupancy on a nontransient, permanent basis.

3. The gross rent paid by the low-income family or individual cannot be more than 30 percent of the qualifying income level for that family or individual. This rental figure includes the cost of utilities, except telephone, in order to qualify for this test.

4. The owner of a low-income project is required to certify to the IRS that in fact the project has complied with the various requirements.

5. The project must meet these requirements for a compliance period of 15 years to qualify for the low-income housing credit. If during the compliance period requirements are not met, then a portion of the credit will have to be recaptured (given back), which will increase the tax liability.

Figuring the Tax Credit

The following is the general formula used to figure the low-income housing tax credit:

Cost of construction or purchase (eligible basis) multiplied by the proportion of eligible basis attributable to low-income units equals the qualified basis multiplied by credit percentage of 9% or 4% in 1987 equals the low-income housing tax credit.

The *eligible basis* of the formula consists of three components which determine the amount of expenditures that qualify for the tax credit:

1. The cost of eligible construction.

2. The cost of rehabilitation expenditures. To qualify these expenditures must average at least $2,000 per low-income housing unit. Cost incurred for rehabilitation during a two-year period from the date the rehabilitation originated can be included.

3. The cost of acquiring an existing project. In order to have the costs of an existing project qualify in the eligible basis, the project and any improvement to it had to have been put into service more than 10 years before the current acquisition. The costs incurred of any rehabilitation expenditures before the end of the first year of the credit period can be included. Minimum rehabilitation expenditures, as described in item 2 above, are not required.

Certain general requirements apply to the eligible expenditures in the above three items. The investment, or tax basis, of the project is included in this amount, while the cost of the land is not. Should the investor claim the rehabilitation tax credit, a reduction in the depreciable basis of the project is factored into the calculation of eligible basis. Expenditures for amenities of certain personal property, such as furniture and fixtures, can be included. The cost of certain tenant facilities can also be included in the eligible basis if no separate fee is charged and the facilities are made available on a comparable basis for all tenants. These include facilities such as parking lots, swimming pools, tennis courts, or other recreational areas. If certain commercial tenants reside in the project, it will still be considered eligible. However, the cost of such nonresidential activity is required to be excluded from the eligible basis calculation. Finally, no portion of the funds derived from any federal grant can be included in the eligible basis.

Now to determine the *proportion of the eligible basis that qualifies.* This step is required to determine the percentage of the eligible basis which can be included in the amount (qualifying basis) on which the low-income credit is calculated. This is accomplished by multiplying the eligible basis by the lower of the two ratios below:

$$\frac{\text{Total number of low-income units}}{\text{Total number of residential units}}$$

or

$$\frac{\text{Floor space of low-income units}}{\text{Total floor space of residential units}}$$

From the above ratios you can only use low-income units that are actually occupied by low-income tenants. The figure for total number of residential units, on the other hand, includes all units, whether they are occupied or not.

In conclusion, before being overwhelmed by the benefits of such a tax credit, carefully consider the limitations, restrictions, and of course the cumbersome bureaucratic red tape involved. In many cases the tax credit for low-income housing will not be available, or if available, will not be worth the bother.

Tax Credit for Rehabilitating Old and Historic Buildings

Tax reform has substantially reduced the benefits and availability of the tax credit associated with renovating certain old and historic buildings. Although these new rules are more restricting than before, the tax credit now available deserves attention because it can be valuable to real estate developers in some situations. Essentially, the tax credit is a two-tier credit which can offset your tax liability on a dollar-for-dollar basis, as follows:

1. Twenty percent tax credit on costs incurred in renovating a building that qualifies as a certified historic structure. For the build-

ing to qualify it must be located in a registered historic district or be listed in the National Register of Historic Places. In addition, the Secretary of the Interior must approve the renovation of the building.

2. Ten percent tax credit on costs incurred in renovating a building that was placed in service before 1936. Only residential property may qualify for the 20 percent certified historic-structure credit. It may not qualify for the 10 percent credit. To qualify for the tax credit the renovation must be "substantial." This means that the qualifying cost spent on the renovation work itself, exclusive of the acquisition costs of building and land or enlarging the building, must be greater than (1) $5,000, or (2) your investment (adjusted tax basis which is cost less depreciation) in the building. These renovation costs must be completed within 24 months. (This qualifying period can be extended under certain circumstances.)

In addition to the above requirements, certain other tests must be met:

- At least 75 percent of the structure's external walls must be retained as either external or internal walls.
- At least 75 percent of the building's internal structural framework, such as beams and load-bearing walls, must be retained.
- At least 50 percent of the structure's external walls must be retained as external walls.

If you claim the tax credit, for the purposes of calculating depreciation the adjusted tax basis of the building must be reduced by the amount of the tax credit. Finally, if the owner of the renovated building agrees, the rehabilitation tax credit can be claimed by the building's tenant. For the tenant to qualify, his unexpired lease term must at least equal the depreciation period for the property, which is 27.5 years for residential property and 31.5 years for nonresidential property.

MISCELLANEOUS TAX AND ADMINISTRATIVE CHANGES

Tax reform has brought about numerous administrative and technical changes relevant to the real estate industry. It is therefore the intent of this section to make you aware of these changes, enabling you to work or communicate more efficiently with your tax adviser.

Registration of Tax Shelters

A tax shelter must be registered with the IRS, and the registration must be no later than the day on which interests in it are first offered for sale to investors. The principal organizer of the shelter is responsible for the filing. However if he fails to do so, another member of the shelter can be responsible.

An investment is considered a tax shelter for registration requirements if the investment's tax shelter ratio for any of the first five years of the investment is greater than 2:1. This ratio is calculated as follows:

$$\frac{\text{Total deductions} + (350\% \times \text{tax credits})}{\text{Investment}}$$

If this ratio is more than 2:1, then the investment qualifies.

Besides the above ratio requirement, the investment is required: (1) to be registered under a federal or state law regulating securities; (2) to be more than, in aggregate, $250,000 and sold to at least five or more investors; or (3) to be sold pursuant to an exemption for registration requiring the filing of a notice with a federal or state agency.

Under registration requirements the seller must provide each investor with the tax shelter identification number issued by the IRS. Then, the investor must report this number on his tax return.

Finally, the IRS can assess penalties for failing to meet these requirements, as follows:

- A 1 percent penalty, or $500, whichever is greater, can be assessed for failing to register a tax shelter.

- A $250 penalty can be assessed for failing to report the tax shelter identification number on your tax return.

- The tax shelter organizer can be assessed a penalty of $50 per failure up to a maximum of $100,000 per year for failing to maintain an investor list.

Reporting Rental Income and Deductions

Rental income and expenses are reported on Schedule E of your tax return. You report the gross amount received, then deduct such expenses as mortgage interest, property taxes, maintenance costs, and depreciation. The net profit is added to your other taxable income. If you realize a loss, you can reduce the amount of your other taxable income within certain limitations. (See passive-loss limitation rules discussed above.)

On the cash basis, you report rental income for the year in which you receive payment.

On the accrual basis, you report rental income for the year in which you are entitled to receive payment. You do not report accrued income if the financial condition of your tenant makes collection doubtful. If you sue for payment, you do not report income until you win a collectible judgment.

Insurance proceeds for loss of rental income because of fire or casualty loss are reported as ordinary income.

Payment by tenant for cancelling a lease or modifying its terms is reported as ordinary income when received. You may deduct expenses realized from the cancellation and any unamortized balance for expenses paid in negotiating the lease.

Security deposits are treated as trust funds and are not reported as income. However, if your tenant breaches the lease agreement, then you are entitled to use the security deposit as rent, at which time you report it as income.

Checklist of Deductions from Rental Income

Real estate taxes. Property taxes are deductible, but special assessments for paving roads, sewers, or other improvements are not. They are added to the cost of the land.

Depreciation. Be sure to deduct depreciation; it is the tax shelter benefit of real estate ownership.

Maintenance expenses. Repairs, pool service, heating, lighting, water, gas, electricity, telephone, and other service costs.

Management expenses. Include the cost of stationery and postage stamps, or the total cost of a management service.

Traveling expenses. These include travel back and forth from properties for repairs or showing vacancies.

Legal expenses. These include the costs incurred while evicting a tenant. Expenses incurred for negotiating long-term leases are considered capital expenditures and deductible over the term of the lease.

Interest expense. This includes interest on mortgages and other indebtedness related to the property.

Advertising expense. This includes the cost of vacancy signs and newspaper advertising.

Insurance expense. This includes the cost of premiums for fire and casualty loss.

Note the difference between repair expenses and an improvement.

Only incidental repair costs and maintenance costs are deductible against rental income. Improvement and replacement costs are treated differently. Improvements or repairs that add value or prolong the life of the property are considered capital improvements and may not be deducted but may be added to the cost basis of the property, and then be depreciated. For example, the cost to repair the roof of a rental property is considered an expense and is deducted against rental income. However, the cost to replace the entire roof is considered an improvement (adds value and prolongs the physical life of the property) and is therefore added to the cost basis of the property and then depreciated.

SUMMARY

Congress designed the 1986 Tax Reform Act with the intention of implementing a doctrine of fairness, and at the same time it attempted to simplify the overall tax system. It did accomplish a certain amount of fairness when it reduced individual tax rates and strictly limited the amount of tax shelter benefits, especially for the very wealthy; however, it did not by any means simplify the tax system, in fact it has been made more complex.

Now under the new regulations since the passage of the Act, special care must be taken by borrowers. Deductions for interest paid on non-mortgage loans depend upon how the borrowed money is used. Under the old law interest was generally deductible no matter how the proceeds from a loan were spent.

Taxpayers who borrow since the 1986 Act must trace how they use the loan proceeds from the day they take it out until the day it is repaid.

Under the new rules, more forms and stricter accounting practices will be required of the taxpayer. In order to comply under the new complex system, the following procedures are suggested to simplify record-keeping and to avoid losing deductions because of improper record-keeping methods:

- Maintain separate accounts for personal, business, and investment use.
- Be sure that debts incurred for investments can be traced to the investment. (Note the 15-day rule: that the taxpayer who spends the proceeds of a loan within 15 days qualifies for the deduction;

however, if the loan proceeds sit longer than 15 days, the IRS will base the deduction eligibility on the first purchase made from the borrowed funds).

- As opposed to other forms of loans, consider home-equity loans, which are fully tax deductible and don't require as much record-keeping.
- Refrain from writing checks on stock margin accounts for purposes other than buying stock.

14 HOW REAL ESTATE CAN GIVE YOU LIFETIME INCOME

Although owning income property can be profitable and fun, these things do not happen without a certain amount of work and effort on your part. I have prepared for you a complete guide to investing in real estate, however it is you who must implement the ideas presented in the text. You are required to do the following: locate the right property to invest in, negotiate with the seller for its purchase, locate tenants, collect rents, handle improvements and repairs, and prepare your income tax returns to maximize the tax shelter benefits.

It is you who must determine whether you are capable of doing the above functions. These are the drawbacks of owning income property. Now consider the advantages.

Real estate, on the average, will appreciate one-and-a-half times the rate of inflation. That's right . . . 1.5 times the rate of inflation. Thus, you have a super hedge against inflation.

Not only, then, is inflation on your side as a real estate investor, but time is also. As time passes, rents can be increased, which means that the property you initially purchased which had little or no cash flow then, can later develop positive cash flow from these increases.

Many property owners who have been fortunate enough to hold on to their properties for a long time are able to live off the net rental income. In other words, income property purchased today with a small down payment will unlikely net a substantial positive cash flow. Yet as time passes, the property appreciates and rents are increased gradually, which over the long term will produce a substantial net income for the owner. Therefore, the longer you own the property, the greater the net income from it becomes. And during the time of ownership you enjoy the tax shelter benefits from the property. In other words, buy all the income property you can when you are young, then enjoy the income benefits when you are old.

Besides the benefits of appreciation, growing income, and tax shelter, you also have a tremendous refinancing benefit. You can periodically refinance your holdings as the market value of your properties increases. Every few years you can refinance certain properties, pulling out cash to reinvest in more properties, or do whatever you want with it.

Still another method of income production occurs when the owner of real estate decides to sell. After owning property for an extended period, the owner will realize a sizable gain from the sale. He has the option of taking all cash from the gain or of accepting a note for his equity in the property. This is ideal for retirees who quit their jobs and sell their properties carrying the financing on a installment sale, and enjoying the income from those monthly checks.

Variations of how real estate can provide income for its owner are almost boundless. But where will you as an individual be as time goes on? That is entirely up to you. You can either be a landlord or a tenant or a homeowner. As a tenant you are only a tiny cog in the great financial wheels of progress that continues to pay rent (which is income to the landlord) just to have a place to live. Or you can join in the general prosperity that is enjoyed by the deserving and elite class of people who call themselves landlords. You can become knowledgeable and experienced about real estate and use this knowledge and, with careful planning, take control of your own future. Even as a homeowner, you have the privilege at day's end to return to your appreciating investment—to that wonderful parcel of earth which belongs solely to you and has oft been called "home, sweet home."

APPENDIX: LAND DESCRIPTION AND MEASUREMENT

The following illustration describes townships within the state of Arizona. Each state within the U.S.A. is similarly described and measured.

Note that the principal meridian runs north and south from border to border of the adjacent states; the baseline runs east and west from border to border.

Each small square noted in the illustration is a township, which is six-miles square. Each township contains 36 sections. The following material will further describe and measure townships and sections.

A TOWNSHIP

- Each township contains 36 sections. Each section is one-mile square.
- The sections within a township are always numbered with section number 1 in the NE corner and section number 36 in the SE corner.
- Perimeter lines of the township are described as follows: lines running north and south are range lines, lines running east and west are township lines. These lines are six miles apart.

Therefore, a township described as "T5N-R1E" would be described as Township 5 North Range 1 East. (The fifth Township North of the Baseline and one Range East of the principal meridian.)

STATE OF ARIZONA

North

Utah

Note: Every state within the USA consists of townships. Each of these small squares represents one township, which is six miles square.

PRINCIPAL MERIDIAN

Colorado River

Salt River

BASELINE

West

Gila River

East

T1N, R32E

California

ARIZONA
Gila and Salt River
Base and Meridian

Mexico

South

A SECTION

- A section is one-mile square and contains 640 acres.
- A section is the smallest area surveyed by the government survey system.
- Individual sections break down into halves and quarters, which in turn break down into halves and quarters, etc.
- A section has 16 parcels of 40 acres each.
- One square acre would measure approximately 209′ × 209′.

ENLARGEMENT OF
INTERSECTION OF BASELINE & MERIDIAN
STATE OF ARIZONA

T6N R6W											T6N R6E
T4N R6W	T4N R5W	T4N R4W	T4N R3W	T4N R2W	T4N R1W	T4N R1E	T4N R2E	T4N R3E	T4N R4E	T4N R5E	T4N R6E
			T3N R3W								
			T2N R3W								
			T1N R3W		T1N R1W	BASELINE					
			T1S R3W		T1S R1W	T1S R1E					
T6S R6W*					MERIDIAN						

*This particular township is "Township 6 South, Range 6 West."

Each square above is a township (6 miles square and containing 36 sections). Note that lines running north and south are range lines. Lines running east and west are township lines. All lines are 6 miles apart.

SECTION 25

The following illustration of Section 25 shows how a section is broken down into smaller areas. The description of a parcel of land begins with the smallest portion first, then each successively larger portion.

TOWNSHIP

A standard township within a county is
6 miles square containing 36 sections.

6	5	4	3	2	1
7	8	9	10	11	12
18	17	16	15	14	13
19	20	21	22	23	24
30	29	28	27	26	25
31	32	33	34	35	36

6 miles

1-section

6 miles

SECTION

40 acres	40 acres	40 acres	40 acres

½ mile

¼ mile

1-mile

1-section

When plotting to a map from a written description, you must read the description backwards (from right to left). What you are doing is locating the largest possible parcel, dividing that into smaller portions, locating one of those portions, then possibly breaking that one into smaller portions, etc. If the particular parcel you wish to describe has an odd shape, then the description would be described in metes and bounds.

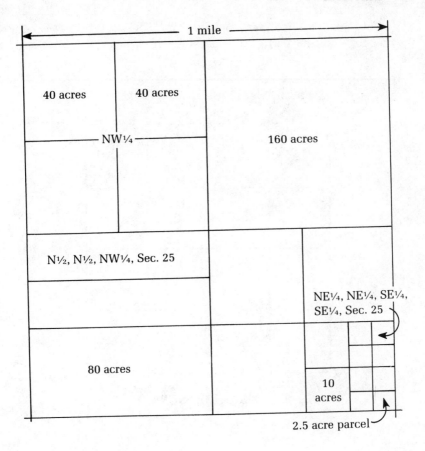

Metes and Bounds

A description using the metes and bounds method is necessary to legally describe odd-shaped parcels. Required are a starting point, directions, and specified distances.

To write a description using this method you begin by establishing the known starting point. Then you trace around the perimeter of the parcel, noting the direction and distance for each leg until you finally return to the original starting point.

For example, in the parcel outlined below, the legal description using metes and bounds would be as follows: "Begin at a point located at the NW corner of Section 5; T4S, R5W, G&SRB&M: thence in a SE direction to SE corner of the NW ¼ of the NW ¼ of Sec. 5; thence ¾ miles South in a straight line to the SW corner of the SE ¼ of the

SW ¼ of Sec. 5; thence West ¼ mile to the SW ¼ of the SW ¼ of Sec. 5; thence 1 mile North in a straight line back to the point of beginning.''

SECTION 5, T4S, R5W, G&SRB&M

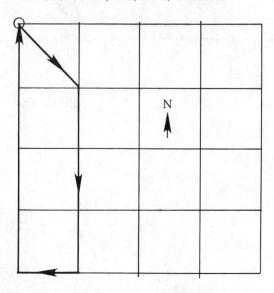

LINEAR MEASURE

1 Link	=	7.92 inches
25 Links	=	1 Rod
1Rod	=	16.5 Feet
100 Links	=	1 Chain
4 Rods	=	1 Chain
66 Feet	=	1 Chain
80 Chains	=	1 Mile
320 Rods	=	1 Mile
5280 Feet	=	1 Mile

SQUARE MEASURE

43,560 square feet	=	1 acre
208. 708′ × 208. 708′	=	1 acre
16 square rods	=	1 square chain
10 square chains	=	1 acre
160 square rods	=	1 acre
640 acres (one section)	=	1 square mile
36 square miles	=	1 township

GLOSSARY OF REAL ESTATE DEFINITIONS

Abandonment The voluntary relinquishment of rights of ownership or another form of interest (an easement) by failure to use the property over an extended period of time.

Absentee landlord A lessor of real property (usually the owner) who does not reside on any portion of the property.

Abstract of title A summary of the conveyances, transfers, and any other data relied on as evidence of title, together with any other elements of record which may impair the title. Still in use in some states, but giving way to the use of title insurance.

Accelerated depreciation Depreciation occurring at a rate faster than the normal rate. This form of depreciation is usually used for special assets for income tax purposes.

Acceleration clause A clause in a mortgage or trust deed giving the lender the right to call all monies owed to be immediately due and payable upon the happening of a certain stated event.

Acceptance Refers to a legal term denoting acceptance of an offer. A buyer offers to buy and the seller accepts the offer.

Access right A right to enter and exit one's property.

Accretion Gradual deposit of soil from a waterway onto the adjoining land. The additional land generally becomes the property of the owner of the shore or bank, except where local statutes specify otherwise.

Accrued depreciation The amount of depreciation accumulated over a period of time in the accounting system for replacement of an asset.

Acknowledgment A formal declaration of execution of a document before an authorized official (usually a notary public) by a person who has executed (signed) a document.

Acre A measure of land, equal to 160 sq. rods (43,560 sq. ft.). An acre is approximately 209' × 209'.

Addendum   Something added. A list or other items added to a document, letter, contract, escrow instructions, etc. Adjustable rate mortgages (ARMs) with an interest rate that can change as often as specified.

Adjusted-cost basis   The value of an asset on the accounting books of a taxpayer which is his original cost plus improvements less depreciation.

Adverse land use   A use of land which causes the surrounding property to lose value, such as a truck terminal adjacent to a residential area.

Adverse possession   A method of acquiring title by open and notorious possession under an evident claim or right. Specific requirements for time of possession usually vary with each state.

Affidavit   A written statement or declaration sworn to or affirmed before some official who has the authority to administer affirmation. An oath.

Agency agreement (listing)   A listing agreement between the seller of real property and a broker wherein the broker's commission is protected against a sale by other agents but not by the principal (seller). Often referred to as a non-exclusive agency listing.

Agent   A person who is authorized to represent or act for another in business matters.

Agreement of sale   A written contract between the buyer and the seller, where both parties are in full agreement on the terms and conditions of the sale.

Alienation   The transfer of property from one person to another.

Alienation clause   A clause within a loan instrument calling for a debt in its entirety upon the transfer of ownership of the secured property. Similar to a "due-on-sale" clause.

All-Inclusive Trust Deed (AITD)   Same as wrap-around mortgage, except a deed of trust is the security instrument instead of a mortgage.

Alluvion   Soil deposited by accretion.

A.L.T.A.   (American Land Title Association).   A group of title insurance companies which issues title insurance to lenders.

Amenities   Attractive or desirable improvements to property, such as a swimming pool or view of the ocean.

Amortization   The liquidation of a financial obligation using regular equal payments on an installment basis.

Appraisal   An estimate and opinion of value; a factual conclusion resulting from an analysis of pertinent data.

Appreciation   Increase in value of property from improvements or the elimination of negative factors.

Appurtenance   Something belonging to the land and conveyed with it, such as buildings, fixtures, and rights.

ARMs See adjustable rate mortgages.

Assemblage Process of acquiring contiguous properties into one overall parcel for a specific use or to increase value of the whole.

Assessed value Value placed on property by the tax assessor.

Assessment The valuation of property for the purpose of levying a tax, or the amount of the tax levied.

Assessor One appointed to assess property for taxation.

Assignment A transfer or making over to another the whole of any property, real or personal, or of any estate or right therein. To assign is to transfer.

Assignee One who receives an assignment. (Assignor: one who owns property assigned.)

Assumption of mortgage The agreement of a buyer to assume the liability of an existing mortgage. Normally, the lender has to approve the new borrower before the existing borrower is released from the liability.

Attachment Seizure of property by court order, usually done in a pending law suit to make property available in case of judgment.

Balance sheet A financial statement that shows the true condition of a business or individual as of a particular date. Discloses assets, liabilities, and net worth.

Balloon payment The final installment paid at the end of the term of a note; used only when preceding installments were not sufficient to pay off the note in full.

Bankruptcy Procedure of federal law to seize the property of a debtor and divide the proceeds among the creditors.

Base and Meridian Imaginary lines used by surveyors to find and describe the location of public or private lands.

Benchmark A mark used by surveyors which is permanently fixed in the ground to denote height of that point in relation to sea level.

Beneficiary The lender involved in a note and trust deed. One entitled to the benefit of a trust.

Bequeath To give or leave personal property by a will.

Bill of sale An instrument used to transfer personal property.

Blanket mortgage (trust deed) A single mortgage, or trust deed, which covers more than one piece of real estate.

Blighted area A declining area where property values are affected by destructive, economic, or natural forces.

Block busting A method of informing a community of the fact that people of a different race or religion are moving into the neighborhood; this will cause property values to drop, thereby enabling homes to be obtained illegally at below market value.

Boardfoot   A unit of measuring lumber. One boardfoot is 12″ × 12″ × 1, ″ or 144 cubic inches.

Bond   An insurance agreement by which one party is insured against loss or default by a third party. In the construction business a performance bond insures the interested party that the contractor will complete the project. A bond can also be a method of financing debt by a government or corporation; the bond is interest-bearing and has priority over stock in terms of security.

Book value   The value of an asset plus improvements less depreciation.

Boot   A term used when trading property. "Boot" will be the additional value given when trading properties in order to equalize values.

Bottom land   Low-lying ground such as a valley. Also low land along a waterway formed by alluvial deposits.

Breach   Violation of an obligation in a contract.

British Thermal Unit (BTU)   Describes the capacity of heating and cooling systems. It is the unit of heat required to raise one pound of water one degree Fahrenheit.

Broker (real estate)   An agent licensed by the state to carry on the business of operating in real estate. He or she usually receives a commission for services of bringing together buyers and sellers, or tenants and landlords.

Building code   A set of stringent laws that control the construction of buildings, design, materials, and other similar factors.

Building line   A line set by law or deed restricting a certain distance from the street line, in front of which an owner cannot build on his lot. Also known as a setback line.

Built-ins   Items that are not movable, such as stoves, ovens, microwave ovens, and dishwashers.

Built-up roof   A form of level roof consisting of layers of roofing materials covered with fine gravel.

Business opportunity   The sale or lease of a business and good will of an existing business enterprise.

Buyers' market   A market condition which occurs in real estate where more homes are for sale than there are interested buyers.

Capital expenditures   Money spent by a business on improvements such as land, building, and machinery.

Capital gains   A term used for income tax purposes which represents the gain realized from the sale of an asset less the purchase price and deductible expenses. (Before the 1986 tax reform, capital gains rules allowed 60% exclusion in taxes on the sale of an asset if it was a capital gain.)

Capitalization   An appraising term used in determining value by considering net-operating income and a percentage of reasonable return on investment.

Capitalization rate   A percentage used by an investor to determine the value of income property through capitalization.

Cash flow   The owner's spendable income after operating expenses and debt service are deducted.

Caveat emptor   A legal phrase meaning "let the buyer beware." The buyer takes the risk when purchasing an item without the protection of warranties.

Chain of title   A history of conveyances and encumbrances affecting the title to real property as far back as records are available.

Chattel   Personal property.

Chattel mortgage   A mortgage on personal property, as distinguished from one on real property.

Client   One who employs another's services, as in an attorney, real estate agent, insurance agent.

Closing   In the sale of real estate it is the final moment when all documents are executed and recorded and the sale is complete. Also a general selling term where a sales person is attempting to sell something and the buyer agrees to purchase.

Closing costs   Incidental expenses incurred with the sale of real property, such as appraisal fees, title insurance, termite report, etc.

Closing statement   A list of the final accounting of all monies of both buyer and seller and prepared by an escrow agent. It notes all costs each must pay at the completion of a real estate transaction.

Cloud on title   An encumbrance on real property which affects the rights of the owner, which often keeps the title from being marketable until the "cloud" is removed.

Collateral security   A separate obligation attached to another contract pledging something of value to guarantee performance of the contract.

Commercial bank   An institution for checking accounts, loans, savings accounts, and other services usually not found in savings and loan associations. Banks are active in installment loans on vehicles and boats and construction financing rather than on long-term real estate financing. See also Institutional lenders.

Common area   That area owned in common by owners of condominiums and planned unit-development homes within a subdivision.

Community property   Both real and personal property accumulated by a husband and wife after marriage.

Compound interest   Interest paid on the original principal and on interest accrued.

Condemnation   A declaration by governing powers that a structure is unfit for use.

Conditional sales contract   A contract for the sale of property where the buyer has possession and use, but the seller retains title until the conditions of the contract have been fulfilled. Also known as a land contract.

Condominium   A system of individual ownership of units in a multi-unit structure where each space is individually owned, but each owner jointly owns the common areas and land.

Conformity, principle of   An appraising term stating that unformity throughout a certain area produces highest value.

Conservator   A court-appointed guardian.

Consideration   Anything of value given to induce someone into entering into a contract.

Construction loan   The short-term financing of improvements on real estate. Once the improvements are completed, a "take-out" loan for a longer term is used to pay off the existing construction loan.

Contingency   A condition upon which a valid contract is dependent. For example, the sale of a house is contingent upon the buyer's obtaining adequate financing.

Contract   An agreement between two or more parties, written or oral, to do or not to do certain things.

Contract of sale   Same as conditional sales contract or a Land Contract.

Conventional loan   A loan made, usually on real estate, which is not backed by the federal agencies of FHA and VA.

Convertible ARMs   Adjustable rate mortgage which can convert to a fixed-rate mortgage.

Conveyance   The transfer of the title to land from one to another.

Cooperative apartment   A building with two or more units in which the unit owners are required to purchase stock in the corporation that owns the property. The coop was a forerunner to the condominium and is not as popular because of the difficulty in financing, since there is no individual ownership of each unit.

Corporation   A legal entity having certain powers and duties of a natural person, together with rights and liabilities of both, distinct and apart from those persons composing it.

Cost approach   A method of appraisal whereby the estimated cost of a structure is calculated, less the land value and depreciation.

Counteroffer   An offer in response to an offer. *A* offers to buy *B*'s house for $80,000, which is listed for $85,000. *B* counteroffers *A*'s offer by stating that he will sell the house to *A* for $81,000. The $81,000 is a counteroffer.

Covenants   Agreements written into deeds and other instruments stating performance or nonperformance of certain acts or noting certain uses or nonuses of the property.

C.P.M.   Certified Property Manager.

CRV (Certificate of Reasonable Value)   An appraisal of real property issued by the Veteran's Administration.

Cul de sac   A dead-end street with a turn-around included.

Current assets   An accounting term representing assets that can readily be converted into cash, as with short-term accounts receivable and common stocks.

Current liabilities   Short-term debts.

D.B.A. (Doing Business As)   A business name or identification.

Dedication   The donation by an owner of private property for public use.

Deed   A written instrument which when executed conveys title of real property.

Default   Failure to fulfill or discharge an obligation, or to perform any act that has been agreed to in writing.

Defendant   The individual or entity whom a civil or criminal action is brought against.

Deferred payments   Payments to begin in the future.

Delivery   The placing of property in the possession of the grantee.

Demise   A transfer of an estate by lease or will.

Demographics   Statistics regarding new business locations appropriate for chain stores.

Density   The amount of crowding together of buildings, people, or other given things.

Depletion   The reduction or loss in value of an asset.

Deposit receipt   The form used to accept the earnest-money deposit to secure the offer for the purchase of real property.

Depreciation   Loss of value of an asset brought about by age (positive deterioration) or functional and economic obsolescence. Percentage reduction of property value year by year for tax purposes.

Depression   That part of a business cycle where unemployment is high, and production and overall purchasing by the public is low. A severe recession.

Deterioration   The gradual wearing away of the building from exposure to the elements. Also referred to as physical depreciation.

Devise   A gift of real estate by will.

Diluvium   A deposit of land left by a flood.

Diminishing returns   An economic theory stating that an increase in capital or manpower will not increase production proportionately (four laborers may do less than four times the work of one laborer; and two laborers may do more than twice the work of one laborer). The return diminishes when production is proportionately less than input.

Directional growth   The path of development of an urban area. Used to determine where future development will be most profitable.

Divided interest   Different interest in the same property, as in interest of the owner, lessee, or mortgagee.

Documentary tax stamps   Stamps affixed to a deed denoting the amount of transfer tax paid.

Domicile   The place where a person has his permanent home.

Double-declining depreciation   An accelerated method of depreciating an asset where double the amount of straight-line depreciation is used, then reduced from the balance.

Dower   The portion of her husband's estate which a wife inherits on his death.

Down payment   Cash or other consideration paid toward a purchase by the buyer, as opposed to that amount which is financed.

Due-on-sale clause   A condition written into a financial instrument which gives the lender the right to require immediate repayment of the unpaid balance if the property is sold without consent of the lender.

Easement   The legal right-of-way that permits an owner to cross another's land so as to get to his or her own property. Easement is appurtenant to the land and thus cannot be sold off separately and must be transferred with the title to the land of which it is part. Other forms of rights and privileges with respect to adjacent or nearby land can be created by agreement and are also called easements to the property.

Economic life   The period over which property will yield a return on the investment.

Economic obsolescence   Loss of useful life and desirability of a property through economic forces, such as change in zoning, changes in traffic flow, etc., rather than deterioration.

Economic rent   The current market rental based on comparable rent for a similar unit.

Effective age   The age of a structure estimated by its condition as opposed to its actual age.

Egress   The right to go out across the land of another.

Elevation   The height above sea level. Architecturally, the view looking at the front of a structure.

Emblements Crops growing on the land.

Eminent domain The right of the government to acquire private property for public use by condemnation. The owner must be fully compensated.

Encroachment Trespass. The building or any improvements partly or wholly on the property of another.

Encumbrance Anything which affects or limits the fee simple title to property, such as mortgages, trust deeds, easements, or restrictions of any kind. Liens are special encumbrances which make the property security for the debt.

Entity An existence or being, as in a corporation or business, rather than an individual.

Entrepreneur An independent business person taking risks for profit, as opposed to a salaried employee working for someone else.

Equity The value that an owner has in property over and above the liens against it. A legal term based on fairness rather than strict interpretation of the law.

Equity build-up The reduction in the difference between property value and the amount of the lien as regular payments are made. The equity increases (builds up) on an amortized loan as the proportion of interest payment gets smaller, causing the amount going toward principal to increase.

Escalation clause A clause in a lease providing for an increase in rent at a future time because of increased costs to lessor, as in cost-of-living index, tax increases, etc.

Escheat The reverting of property to the state in the absence of heirs.

Escrow A neutral third party who carries out the provisions of an agreement between two or more parties.

Estate The ownership interest of a person in real property. Often used to describe a large home with spacious grounds. Also a deceased person's property.

Estate for years Any estate for a specific period of time. A lease.

Exclusive right-to-sell listing A written contract between agent and owner where the agent has the right to collect a commission if the listed property is sold by anyone during the terms of agreement.

Executor The person appointed in a will to carry out the terms of the will.

Face value The value stated on the face of notes, mortgages, etc., without consideration of any discounting.

Fair market value That price a property will bring given that both buyer and seller are fully aware of market conditions and comparable properties.

Feasibility survey A study of an area prior to development of a project in order to determine if the project will be successful.

Federal Deposit Insurance Corporation (F.D.I.C.) The federal corporation which insures bank depositors against loss up to a specified amount, currently $100,000.

Federal Home Loan Bank Board The board which charters and regulates Federal Savings and Loan Associations and Federal Home Loan Banks.

Federal Home Loan Banks Regulated by the Federal Home Loan Bank Board. Currently 11 regional branches where banks, savings and loans, insurance companies, or similar institutions may join the system and borrow for the purpose of making available home-financing money. Its purpose is to make a permanent supply of financing available for home loans.

Federal Savings and Loan Insurance Corporation (F.S.L.I.C.) A federal corporation which insures deposits in savings and loan associations up to a specified amount, currently $125,000.

Fee simple Ownership of title to property without any limitation, which can be sold, left at will, or inherited.

FHA (Federal Housing Administration) The federal agency that insures first mortgages on homes (and other projects), enabling lenders to extend more lenient terms to borrowers.

FHLMC (Freddie Mac) Federal Home Loan Mortgage Corporation. A federal agency that purchases first mortgages from members of the Federal Reserve System and the Federal Home Loan Bank system.

Fiduciary A person in a position of trust and confidence, as between principal and broker; broker as fiduciary owes loyalty to the principal, which cannot be breached under rules of agency.

First mortgage A mortgage having priority over all other voluntary liens against a specific property.

Fixtures Items, such as plumbing, electrical fixtures, etc., affixed to buildings or land usually in such a way that they cannot be removed without damage to themselves or the property.

FNMA (Fannie Mae) Federal National Mortgage Association. A private corporation that purchases first mortgages at discounts.

Foreclosure Procedure where property pledged for security for a debt is sold at public auction to pay the debt in the event of default in payment and terms.

Free and clear A specific property has no liens, especially voluntary liens, against it.

Front footage The linear measurement along the front of a parcel. That portion of the parcel which fronts the street or walkway.

Functional obsolescence Loss in value due to out-of-date or poorly designed equipment while newer equipment and structures have been invented since its construction.

GEMs   Growing equity mortgages which increase in payment over a specified term. Increases are applied directly to principal reduction.

GNMA (Ginnie Mae)   Government National Mortgage Association. Purchases first mortgages at discounts, similar to that of FNMA.

GPMs   Graduated payment mortgages which increase in payment over their term.

Graduated lease   A lease which provides for rental adjustments, often based upon future determination of the cost-of-living index. Used for the most part in long-term leases.

Grant   A transfer of interest in real property, such as an easement.

Grantee   One to whom the grant is made.

Grantor   The one who grants the property or its rights.

Gross income   Total scheduled income from property before any expenses are deducted.

Gross-income multiplier   A general appraising rule of thumb which when multiplied by the gross annual income of a property will estimate the market value. For example, the property sells for 7.2 times the gross.

Gross lease   A lease obligating the lessor to pay all or part of the expenses incurred on a leased property.

Ground lease   A lease of vacant land.

Ground rent   Rent paid for vacant land.

Hardwood   Wood, such as oak, maple, and walnut, used for interior finish, as opposed to certain other soft woods.

Highest and best use   An appraisal term for the use of land which will bring the highest economic return over a given time.

Homeowners association   An association of homeowners within a community formed to improve and maintain the quality of the community. An association formed by the developer of condominiums or planned-unit developments.

Homestead   A declaration by the owner of a home that protects the home against judgments up to specified amounts provided by certain state laws.

Hypothecate   To give a thing as security without giving up possession of it, as with mortgaging real property.

Impound account   A trust account held for the purpose of paying taxes, insurance, and other periodic expenses incurred with real property.

Improvements   A general term to describe buildings, roads, and utilities which have been added to raw (unimproved) land.

Inflation   The increase in an economy over its true or natural growth. Usually identified with rapidly increasing prices.

Installment note   A note that provides for regular monthly payments to be paid on the date specified in the instrument.

Institutional lenders   Banks, savings and loans, or other businesses who make loans to the public during their ordinary course of business, as opposed to individuals who fund loans.

Instrument   A written legal document.

Intangible value   The good will or well-advertised name of an established business.

Interim loan   A short-term loan usually for real estate improvements during the period of construction.

Intestate   A person who dies without having made a will.

Intrinsic value   The value of a thing by itself without certain aspects which will add value to some and not to others, as with a vintage Rolls Royce, which might have value to a car collector, but to few others.

Investment   The laying out of money in the purchase of some form of property intending to earn a profit.

Involuntary lien   A lien that attaches to property without consent of the owner, such as tax liens as opposed to voluntary liens (mortgages).

Joint tenancy   Joint ownership by two or more persons with right of survivorship. Upon the death of a joint tenant, the interest does not go to the heirs but to the remaining joint tenants.

Junior mortgage   A mortgage lower in priority than a first mortgage, such as second and third mortgages.

Land Contract   A contract for the sale of property where the buyer has possession and use, but the seller retains title until certain conditions of the contract have been fulfilled. Same as a conditional sales contract.

Land grant   A gift of public land by the federal government.

Landlord   The owner of rented property.

Lease   A contract between the owner of real property, called the lessor, and another person or party referred to as the lessee, covering the conditions by which the lessee may occupy and use the property.

Lease with option to purchase   A lease where the lessee has the option to purchase the leased property, the terms of which must be set forth in the lease.

Legacy   A gift of personal property by will.

Legal description   The geographical identification of a parcel of land.

Legatee   One who receives personal property from a will.

Lessee   One who contracts to rent property under a specified lease.

Lessor   An owner who contracts into a lease with a tenant (lessee).

Leverage   The use of a small amount of cash to control a much greater value of assets.

Liability   A term covering all types of debts and obligations.

Lien   An encumbrance against real property for money as in taxes, mortgages, and judgments.

Life estate   An estate in real property for the life of a person.

Limited partnership   A partnership of one or more general partners which operates a business along with one or more limited partners who contribute capital. This arrangement limits certain of the partner's liability to the amount of money contributed.

Liquidate   Disposal of property or assets or the settlement of debts.

Lis pendens   A recorded legal notice showing pending litigation of real property. Anyone acquiring an interest in such property after the recording of *lis pendens* could be bound to the outcome of the litigation.

Listing   A contract between owner and broker to sell the owner's real property.

Long-term capital gain   Prior to the 1986 tax reform it was a preferential tax treatment excluding 60 percent of the gain incurred on the sale of an asset held for at least six months.

M.A.I. (Member Appraisal Institute)   A designation issued to a member of the American Institute of Real Estate Appraisers after meeting specific qualifications.

Maintenance reserve   Money held in reserve to cover anticipated maintenance expenses.

Marketable title   A saleable title free of objectionable liens or encumbrances.

Market-data approach   An appraisal method to determine value by comparing similar properties to the subject property.

Market value   The price a buyer will pay and a seller will accept, both being fully informed of market conditions.

Master plan   A comprehensive zoning plan to allow a city to grow in an orderly manner.

Mechanics lien   A lien created by statute on a specific property for labor or materials contributed to an improvement on that property.

Metes and Bounds   A legal description used in describing boundary lines.

M.G.I.C. (Mortgage Guaranty Insurance Corporation)   Private corporation that insures mortgage loans.

Mineral rights   Ownership of the minerals beneath the ground. The owner of mineral rights doesn't necessarily own the surface land.

Moratorium   Temporary suspension of the enforcement of liability for a debt.

Mortgage   An instrument by which property is hypothecated to secure the payment of a debt.

Mortgage broker   A person who, for a fee, brings together the lender with the borrower. Also known as a loan broker.

Mortgagee   One who loans the money and receives the mortgage.

Mortgagor   One who borrows on his property and gives a mortgage as security.

Multiple Listing Service (MLS)   A listing taken by a member of an organization of brokers, whereby all members have an opportunity to find a buyer.

Net income   Gross income less operating expenses.

Net lease   A lease requiring tenant to pay all or part of the expenses on leased property in addition to the stipulated rent.

Net listing   A listing whereby agent may retain as compensation all sums received over and above a net price to the owner. Illegal in some states.

Net worth   Total assets less liabilities of an individual, corporation, or business.

Nonexclusive listing   A listing where the agent has an exclusive listing with respect to other agents; however, owner may sell the property without being liable for a commission.

Notary public   One who is authorized by federal or local government to attest authenetic signatures and administer oaths.

Note   A written instrument acknowledging a debt and promising payment.

Notice to quit   A notice issued by landlord to the tenant to vacate rented property, usually for nonpayment of rent or breach of contract.

Offer   A presentation to form a contract or agreement.

Open listing   An authorization given by an owner to a real estate agent to sell the owner's property. Open listings may be given to more than one agent without liability, and only the one who secures a buyer on satisfactory terms gets paid a commission.

Operating expenses   Expenses relevant to income-producing property, such as taxes, management, utilities, insurance, and other day-to-day costs.

Option   A right given, for consideration, to purchase or lease property upon stipulated terms within a specific period of time.

Passive activity   New definition under the 1986 tax reform. A passive activity is any activity that involves the conduct of any trade or business in which you do not materially participate. Any rental activity will be a passive activity even if you materially participate. Prior to the tax reform, passive losses could offset other forms of income; subsequent to the act, the taxpayer is limited to this benefit.

Percentage lease   A lease on property where normally a minimum specified rent is paid or a percentage of gross receipts of the lessee is paid, whichever is higher.

Personal property   Property which is not real property (real estate).

Planned development   Five or more individually owned lots where one or more other parcels are owned in common or there are reciprocal rights in one or more other parcels; subdivision.

Plat map   A map or plan of a specified parcel of land.

Plat book   A book containing plat maps of a certain area.

P.M.I. (Private Mortgage Insurance)   Insurance which covers a portion of the first mortgage allowing the lender to offer more lenient terms to a borrower.

Point   One percent. A one-point fee often charged by the lender to originate the loan. On FHA and VA loans, the seller pays points to accommodate the loan.

Power of attorney   An instrument authorizing a person to act as the agent of the person granting the power.

Preliminary title report   The report of condition of the title before a sale or loan transaction. Once completed, a title insurance policy is issued.

Prepayment penalty   A penalty within a note, mortgage, or trust deed, imposing a penalty if the debt is paid in full before the end of its terms.

Prime lending rate   The most favorable interest rate charged by an institutional lender to its best customers.

Principal   The employer of an agent. Also, the amount of debt, not including interest.

Proration of taxes   To divide or prorate the taxes equally or proprortionately to time of use.

Purchase agreement   An agreement between buyer and seller denoting price and terms of the sale.

Pyramid   To build an estate by multiple acquistions of properties using the initial properties for a base for further investment.

Quitclaim deed   A deed used to remove clouds on a title by relinquishing any right, title, or interest that the grantor may have.

Realtor   A real estate broker holding membership in a real estate board affiliated with the National Association of Realtors.

Redemption   The buying back of one's property after it has been lost through foreclosure. Payment of delinquent taxes after sale to the state.

R.E.I.T. (Real Estate Investment Trust)   A method of group investment with certain tax advantages, although it is governed by federal and state laws.

Rent   Consideration, usually money, for the occupancy and use of real property.

Replacement-cost method   A method of appraisal to determine value by determining an exact replica.

Request for notice of default   A request by a lender which is recorded for notification in the case of default by a loan with priority over other junior loans.

Right of survivorship   Right to acquire the interest of a deceased joint owner. Distinguishing characteristic of joint tenancy.

Right-of-way   A privilege given by the owner of a property to give another the right to pass over his land.

Riparian rights   The right of a landowner to water on, under, or adjacent to the land owned.

Sale-leaseback   A sale of a subsequent lease from the buyer back to the seller.

Savings and Loan Association   An institution which retains deposits for savers and lends out these deposits for home loans.

Secondary financing   A junior loan or second in priority to a first mortgage or trust deed.

Security deposit   Money given to a landlord by the tenant to secure performance of the rental agreement.

Sellers' market   A time when there are more buyers than sellers.

Separate property   Property owned by husband or wife which is not community property. Property acquired before marriage or by a gift, will, or inheritance.

Severalty   An estate held by one person alone, an individual right. The term is misleading as it does not mean several persons own it. Distinguished from joint tenancy.

Sheriff's deed   Deed given by court order in connection with the sale of a property to satisfy a judgment.

Single-family residence   A general term to distinguish a house from an apartment house, a condominium, or a planned-unit development.

Special assessment   Legal charge against real estate by public authority to pay the cost of public improvements (i.e., sewers) by which the property is benefitted.

Speculator   One who buys property with the intent of selling it quickly at a profit.

SRA (Society of Real Estate Appraisers)   One is designated a Senior Residential Appraiser after receiving experience and education in the field of appraising.

Straight-line depreciation   Reducing the value for tax purposes over an extended period of time by equal increments.

Straight note   A nonamortized note promising to repay a loan, signed by the debtor and including the amount, date due, and interest rate.

Subdivision   A division of one parcel of land into smaller lots.

Subject-to mortgage   When a buyer takes title to real property "subject-to mortgage," buyer is not responsible to the holder of the note. The original maker of the note is not released from the liability of the note and the most the new buyer can lose in foreclosure is the equity in the property.

Sublease   A lease given by a lessee.

Syndicate   A group of investors who invest in one or more properties through a partnership, corporation, or trust.

Take-out commitment   Agreement by a lender to have available a long-term loan over a specified time once construction is completed.

Tax base   The assessed value multiplied by the tax rate to determine the amount of tax due.

Tax sale   A sale of property, usually at auction, for nonpayment of taxes assessed against it.

Tenancy in common   Ownership by two or more persons who hold an undivided interest without right of survivorship.

Tenant   The holder of real property under a rental agreement. Also referred to as a lessee.

Tender   An offer of money, usually in satisfaction of a claim or demand.

Tenements   All rights in land which pass with the conveyance of the land. Also commonly refers to certain groups of multiple dwellings.

Testator   A person who leaves a legally valid will at his death.

Tight money   A condition in the money market in which demand for the use of money exceeds the available supply.

Timeshare   Shared ownership wherein the owners are allowed limited use of a property.

Title insurance   Insurance written by a title company to protect the property owner against loss if title is imperfect.

Topography   Character of the surface of land. Topography may be level, rolling, or mountainous.

Township   A territorial subdivision six miles long, six miles wide, and containing 36 sections, each one-mile square.

Tract house   A house similar to other homes within a subdivision and built by the same developer, as opposed to a custom home built to owner specifications.

Trade fixtures   Personal property of a business which is attached to the property, but can be removed upon the sale of the property.

Trust deed   An instrument which conveys legal title of a property to a trustee to be held pending fulfillment of an obligation, usually the repayment of a loan to a beneficiary (lender).

Trustee   One who holds bare legal title to a property in trust for another to secure performance of a debt obligation.

Trustor   The borrower of money secured by a trust deed.

Unimproved land   Land in its natural state without structures on it.

Unlawful detainer   An action of law to evict a person or persons illegally occupying real property.

Usury   Interest rate charged on a loan in excess of that permitted by law.

Variable interest rate   A fluctuating interest rate that can go up or down depending on the market rate.

Vendee   A purchaser or buyer.

Vendor   A seller.

Vested   Bestowed upon someone or secured by someone, such as title to property.

Voluntary lien   A voluntary lien by the owner, such as a mortgage, as opposed to an involuntary lien (i.e., taxes).

Waive   To relinquish, or abandon. To forgo a right to enforce or require anything.

Wrap-around mortgage   A second mortgage which is subordinate to but includes the face value of the first mortgage. Also referred to as an All-Inclusive Trust Deed, or AITD.

Zoning   Act of city or county authorities specifying the types of use for which property may be used in specific areas.

INDEX